Understanding Chronic Kidney Disease

Other books from M&K include:

The Clinician's Guide to Chronic Disease Management for Long-Term Conditions: A cognitive-behavioural approach
ISBN: 9781905539154

Therapy Skills for Healthcare: An introduction to brief psychological techniques
ISBN: 9781905539581

Developing Advanced Assessment Skills: Patients with Long Term Conditions
ISBN: 9781905539185

The Primary Care Guide to Mental Health
ISBN: 9781905539109

My Health, My Faith, My Culture: A guide for healthcare practitioners
ISBN: 9781905539802

Identification and Treatment of Alcohol Dependency
ISBN: 9781905539161

Routine Blood Results Explained
ISBN: 9781905539383

Understanding Chronic Kidney Disease

a guide for the non-specialist

Robert Lewis MD FRCP

Understanding Chronic Kidney Disease: a guide for the non-specialist
Dr Robert Lewis

ISBN: 9781905539-74-1

First published 2012

British Library Cataloguing in Publication Data
A catalogue record for this book is available from the British Library

Notice

Clinical practice and medical knowledge constantly evolve. Standard safety precautions must be followed, but, as knowledge is broadened by research, changes in practice, treatment and drug therapy may become necessary or appropriate. Readers must check the most current product information provided by the manufacturer of each drug to be administered and verify the dosages and correct administration, as well as contraindications. It is the responsibility of the practitioner, utilising the experience and knowledge of the patient, to determine dosages and the best treatment for each individual patient. Any brands mentioned in this book are as examples only and are not endorsed by the publisher. Neither the publisher nor the authors assume any liability for any injury and/or damage to persons or property arising from this publication.

To contact M&K Publishing write to:
M&K Update Ltd · The Old Bakery · St. John's Street
Keswick · Cumbria CA12 5AS
Tel: 01768 773030 · Fax: 01768 781099
publishing@mkupdate.co.uk
www.mkupdate.co.uk

Designed and typeset by Mary Blood
Printed in England by H&H Reeds, Penrith

Contents

Figures

Tables

About the author

Robert Lewis has been a Consultant Renal Physician at the Wessex Regional Renal and Transplant Service, Portsmouth, UK, for 15 years. He qualified from Westminster Medical School and received his renal training in London (at St Bartholomew's Hospital, Kings College Hospital, and Guys Hospital). He was Clinical Director of his unit for seven years and has held executive roles for the major national renal organisations. He has great practical experience in educating primary care practitioners on CKD and was a founder member of the CKD Forum, which aims to improve the interface between primary and secondary care in the management of CKD. He is currently a member of the guideline development group for forthcoming NICE guidance on the diagnosis and management of chronic kidney disease.

Author's note: Some of the data reported here have been supplied by the UK Renal Registry of the Renal Association. The interpretation and reporting of these data are the responsibility of the author and should in no way be seen as an official policy or interpretation of the UK Renal Registry or the Renal Association.

For William and Georgina

Why chronic kidney disease has become such an important issue

'I never bothered to learn about renal disease because I never wanted to be a nephrologist.'

Anonymous senior house officer, Portsmouth, 2005

Prior to 2006, chronic kidney disease (CKD) was very definitely an issue for the specialist. Should a primary care physician chance upon a patient whose blood tests suggested impaired kidney function, a referral was immediately sent to the local nephrologist, who would investigate, try to establish the underlying cause and thereafter keep the patient under regular review in the hospital outpatient clinic. The patient's general practitioner was encouraged not to interfere, but would occasionally receive a letter from a transient renal senior house officer to say that the patient was stable and would be reviewed in the renal clinic in six months' time. This system guaranteed that patients were never seen by the same junior doctor twice, and no one had the confidence to discharge them.

Of the patients with CKD under specialist follow-up, a small fraction might progress to the stage where they required renal replacement therapy in the form of dialysis or transplantation. Once they were receiving these modalities of treatment, the GP was effectively excluded from the process and patients were warned not to seek medical attention from anyone who did not work in their renal unit. GPs learned their lesson well, and knew not to dabble with (what were now) the renal unit's patients. However, this cosy arrangement has now become unsustainable.

Why primary care became involved in managing CKD

The major pressures which led to the involvement of primary care in managing patients with CKD were the need to save money and the emergence of a new understanding of the epidemiology and relevance of CKD. This can be summarised under three broad headings.

1. The need to reduce the amount of money spent on dialysis

Since the 1980s, there had been a huge increase in the number of patients on renal replacement programmes (see Figure 1.1). As dialysis costs between £20,000 and £30,000 per patient per year (depending on modality), any intervention that might lead to a decrease in demand was clearly economically desirable. In order to have any impact on the prevalence of end-stage kidney disease, management of CKD would need to be initiated at the earliest stage. Accordingly, the NHS needed: (i) a means of identifying people at risk of developing CKD; (ii) a systematic targeted screening programme; and (iii) early implementation of measures to reduce the rate of progression.

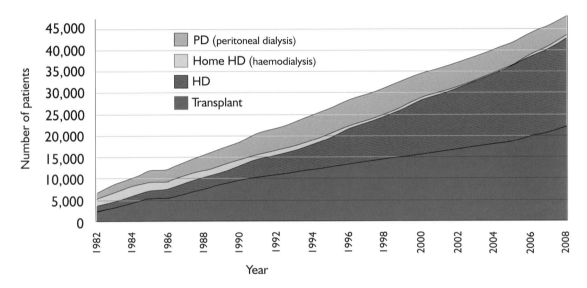

Figure 1.1 *Growth in prevalent patients by modality in the United Kingdom 1982–2008 (UK Renal Registry 13th Annual Report, 2011). Note that the growth in the prevalence of transplantation has not kept pace with the overall growth in patients with end-stage kidney disease. This shortfall has largely been taken up by hospital-based haemodialysis – an expensive alternative.*

As primary care was becoming increasingly proficient at identifying people with hypertension and diabetes (both of which are associated with CKD progression), it was a small step to add monitoring of CKD to this list. Moreover, effective management of disease progression could easily be incorporated into existing primary-care-based public health programmes. It therefore seemed that primary care was ideally placed to make a favourable impact on the prevalence of end-stage kidney disease and thereby stem the growth of the dialysis population.

2. New appreciation of the prevalence of CKD

Large population studies indicated that early CKD (i.e. before dialysis is inevitable) may be a major public health issue. Far from being a niche specialty concern, it appeared that about 10% of the adult population had CKD and that most of this was undiagnosed. Several authors spoke of an 'epidemic of CKD'. In addition to being a risk factor for kidney failure and dialysis, CKD was now seen as a major independent risk factor for the development of cardiovascular disease. Since general practitioners were already heavily involved in cardiovascular risk modification, they needed to know about this hitherto unrecognised risk factor and deal with it in the context of public health as a whole.

3. New healthcare policy

A new guiding principle of NHS reform began to emerge: that patient care should be shifted, as much as possible, away from hospitals and into the community. This arrangement came to be considered more convenient for patients and less demanding of financial resources. During this time, renal units themselves were struggling to keep up with the demands placed upon them by a rising number of patients requiring renal replacement therapy. With resources stretched, it seemed sensible to identify those patients who derived the least benefit from an expensive, high-tech renal unit and to discharge them to their general practitioners with clear instructions on how they should be managed. And if these individuals could be managed in primary care, so too could newly identified patients with similar low-tech medical requirements. The days of renal units accumulating patients with CKD for six-monthly review by a junior doctor were at an end. From now on the GPs would need to take over.

Education and engagement of primary care: NSF, QOF and NICE

Under the influence of the factors described above, in 2005 the Department of Health published *The National Service Framework for Renal Services Part 2: Chronic Kidney Disease, Acute Renal Failure and End of Life Care*. This policy document required a *volte face* in existing management pathways. Instead of serendipitous identification of CKD, followed by immediate referral to a specialist, GPs were now expected to set up systematic programmes to identify CKD and manage it in the community. To facilitate this change, certain indicators relating to CKD were simultaneously incorporated into the Quality and Outcomes Framework (QOF), which determined remuneration to primary care practices. Exactly how the QOF functions is outside the remit of this book, but essentially points are awarded to primary care practices for achieving a specified outcome in a given percentage of their patients. Attainment of these points determines the flow of income to the practice. Table 1.1 shows the QOF points relevant to CKD.

Table 1.1 *Indicators related to chronic kidney disease in the Quality and Outcomes Framework (QOF) of the General Medical Services (GMS) contract.*

Indicator	Points	Payment stages
Records		
CKD 1 The practice can produce a register of patients aged 18 years and over with CKD (US National Kidney Foundation: stage 3 to 5 CKD).	6	—
Management		
CKD 2 The percentage of patients on the CKD register whose notes have a record of blood pressure in the previous 15 months.	6	40–90%
CKD 3 The percentage of patients on the CKD register in whom the last blood pressure reading, measured in the previous 15 months, is 140/85mmHg or less.	11	40–70%
CKD 5 The percentage of patients on the CKD register with hypertension and proteinuria who are treated with an ACE inhibitor or angiotensin II receptor blocker (unless a contraindication or adverse effect is recorded).	9	40–80%
CKD 6 The percentage of patients on the CKD register whose notes have a record of a urinary albumin:creatinine ratio (or protein:creatinine ratio) test in the previous 15 months.	6	40–80%
Smoking 3 The percentage of patients with any or any combination of the following conditions: coronary heart disease, stroke or TIA, hypertension, diabetes, COPD, CKD, asthma, schizophrenia, bipolar affective disorder or other psychoses who smoke, whose notes record smoking status within the previous 15 months.	30	40–90%
Smoking 4 The percentage of patients with any or any combination of the following conditions: coronary heart disease, stroke or TIA, hypertension, diabetes, COPD, CKD, asthma, schizophrenia, bipolar affective disorder or other psychoses who smoke, whose notes contain a record that smoking cessation advice or referral to a specialist service, where available, has been offered within the previous 15 months.	30	40–90%

Almost overnight and with very little warning, GPs were faced with new responsibility for a disease (now defined by an unfamiliar test, the estimated GFR), which had always been the preserve of the local renal unit. What is more, their new employment contract (and thus their income) relied on them managing it according to defined standards.

Nephrologists realised that primary care practitioners would require some easily understood guidelines to increase understanding of what was required. Most renal units wrote their own guidelines and provided resources to their local GPs, but the need for consistent national guidelines was obvious. Accordingly, in 2008, the National Institute of Clinical Excellence (NICE) published *Guideline 73: Early Identification and Management of Chronic Kidney Disease in Adults in Primary and Secondary Care,* which provided an accepted standard for how CKD should be managed in a primary care setting. It recommended that patients at high risk of having unrecognised CKD should be targeted for testing.

NICE guidance on situations in which patients should be routinely tested for the presence of CKD (note that old age and obesity are not included)

- Diabetes
- Hypertension
- Cardiovascular disease (ischaemic heart disease, chronic heart failure, peripheral vascular disease and cerebral vascular disease)
- Structural renal tract disease, renal calculi or prostatic hypertrophy
- Multisystem diseases with potential kidney involvement – for example, systemic lupus erythematosus
- Family history of stage 5 CKD or hereditary kidney disease
- Opportunistic detection of haematuria or proteinuria.

Once CKD was identified, the NICE guideline described how the condition should be effectively managed in primary care, and when patients should be referred for specialist input. The guideline had the virtue of clarity, but it recognised that robust evidence to support some of the recommendations was lacking. As evidence relating to management of CKD continues to accumulate, other organisations have developed their own guidelines, notably the Renal Association in 2010 and the international organisation Kidney Disease Improving Global Outcomes (KDIGO) in 2012. NICE itself is in the process of renewing its 2008 advice, and is likely to change some of its previous recommendations.

Why it is so important for primary care practitioners to know about CKD

Since 2006, the management of CKD has become embedded in routine primary care practice. Whilst there is great variability in the success with which practices identify patients with CKD and place them on their CKD register, it is generally accepted that GPs have made great strides in assimilating this new responsibility. Nonetheless, as detection of individuals meeting the necessary criteria for a diagnosis of CKD has increased, one hears new questions from general practitioners on a regular basis – 'Surely these apparently well, elderly patients with low eGFRs can't *all* have significant major organ failure?' 'Do these osteoporotic ladies in the nursing home *really* benefit from having their blood pressure lowered to 130/70?' 'Since the holiday insurance company is going to quadruple her premiums, is it *really* in the interests of an apparently healthy lady to be told she has CKD stage 3 (not merely stage 1 or 2 but STAGE THREE, how worrying!)?'

There is no simple answer to these questions – certainly nothing evidence-based that can be slipped into a palatable guideline. It is therefore necessary for all healthcare professionals to develop an *understanding* of the means by which CKD is diagnosed and how it can be managed. CKD is now considered a greater public health issue than was previously thought, and there must be a commensurate improvement in the level of understanding of renal disease within the mainstream of basic medical knowledge. Without this knowledge, we are likely to end up with misinformed patients, inappropriate referral to specialists and poor use of precious financial resources.

What is the purpose of this book?

The anonymous medical senior house officer quoted at the start of this chapter was (I hope) the last of a generation who were conditioned to send all renal issues unquestioningly up the line, into the eager arms of the nephrologist. We all know this is bad medicine. His successors will need a clinically based, practical understanding of how to diagnose and manage kidney disease (and what this means for the patient). What no one requires is to be force-fed tubular pathophysiology, podocyte molecular biology or the histology of glomerulonephritis. All these aspects are now covered in renal postgraduate courses; and all of them are, to the non-specialist, stupefyingly boring and completely irrelevant.

This book simply aims to increase understanding of what lies behind the recent plethora of guidelines, protocols and recommendations. It also sets out to fill the gap between the instructions in these documents and the questions patients ask in the clinical arena. It is not intended to be comprehensive (there are any number of nephrology textbooks available for those inclined to read them), and it will ignore those items that are of no practical value to the non-specialist. Armed with this deeper understanding, healthcare professionals without specialist training in nephrology should be sufficiently informed to be able to manage renal disease with greater safety, effectiveness and efficiency.

2

The definition and classification of CKD

Chronic kidney disease is present when either the excretory capacity of the kidneys is reduced or there is proteinuria. The following chapters will describe how these variables are measured in clinical practice. However, it is convenient to start with the currently accepted definition and classification of CKD.

Defining CKD

CKD is present when *either*:
The MDRD-derived estimated glomerular filtration rate (eGFR) is less than 60ml/min on at least two occasions over a period of no less than 90 days

or:

The urine albumin to creatinine ratio (ACR) is greater than 30mg/mmol or the urine protein to creatinine ratio (PCR) is greater than 50mg/mmol.

The terms used in these definitions will be explained later. Clinicians usually remember that reduced eGFR indicates CKD. However, as we shall see, the presence of proteinuria is also very important – perhaps more important – in its consequences for the patient.

Classifying CKD

The classification of CKD in current clinical use requires some explanation. Some years ago, the US National Kidney Foundation Kidney Disease Outcomes Quality Initiative (NKF-KDOQI) classified CKD by dividing it into five stages defined by direct measurement of glomerular filtration rate (GFR). Stage 1 denoted patients with persistent proteinuria or haematuria or structural abnormalities (such as polycystic kidneys or renal asymmetry), in whom renal excretory function was unimpaired (GFR>90ml/min). Stages 2–5 were each defined by the extent of GFR decline. Stage 5 CKD was used to signify established renal failure, also called end-stage renal disease (ESRD).

With the advent of estimated GFR (derived from a formula, rather than direct measurement), it was considered convenient to use the same classification, and GFR was replaced with eGFR. This classification was adopted in the United Kingdom in 2006, following the publication of the Renal National Service Framework.

However, simply replacing GFR with eGFR in the NKF-KDOQI classification presents problems. It was subsequently shown that one could not be confident that the eGFR was pathologically reduced until it was below 60ml/min (hence this level is used in the definition of CKD given at the start of this chapter). The classification designates this level of eGFR as CKD stage 3, so it followed that individuals with CKD 1–2 had excretory function that might be normal (or might not – one couldn't reliably tell). Furthermore, population-based studies indicated that patients with early-stage 3 CKD (eGFR 45–60ml/min) had very little risk of developing end-stage renal failure, although they *did* have a higher than normal chance of developing cardiovascular disease if they were younger than 75 years old. *Post hoc*, stage 3 CKD was therefore divided into stages A and B to reflect this difference.

Numerous studies have shown the impact of proteinuria on prognosis – both renal and cardiovascular. Indeed, it may be more important than eGFR alone. The classification therefore clearly needed some means of identifying proteinuric patients at all stages of CKD. For this reason, the suffix 'P' was attached at each stage when there was significant proteinuria. For reasons that will be discussed in Chapter 5, 'significant' proteinuria is said to be present when the ACR is greater than 30mg/mmol or the PCR is greater than 50mg/mmol. Note that proteinuria at a lower level than this is termed microalbuminuria. This can still be 'significant' in some circumstances, as we shall see, but it does not enter the CKD classification.

This is how we now arrive at the accepted classification shown in Table 2.1. As an example, a patient with an eGFR of 50ml/min with a urine ACR of 60mg/mmol is classified as being at stage 3aP. Some specialists distinguish between patients at stage 5 CKD who have started dialysis by adding the suffix D (i.e. stage 5D). The classification cannot be meaningfully applied to transplant recipients.

Table 2.1 *Classification of CKD, based on NICE 2008.*

Stage of CKD	Estimated GFR
Stage 1	>90ml/min with urine abnormality or abnormal renal anatomy
Stage 2	60–89ml/min with urine abnormality or abnormal renal anatomy
Stage 3a	45–59ml/min
Stage 3b	30–44ml/min
Stage 4	15–29ml/min
Stage 5	<15ml/min or dialysis dependent

The suffix P at each stage denotes the presence of proteinuria (ACR>30 or PCR>50).

Many people are of the opinion that this classification system for CKD does not easily lend itself to clinical application. However, it has been adopted internationally and is widely used in research and healthcare audit. The Quality and Outcomes Framework (QOF) used in UK general practice is an example of this.

As a rule of thumb, the best way to apply the accepted classification of CKD to clinical management is as follows:

- **Stages 1–3a**: manage predominantly to reduce cardiovascular risk

- **Stages 3b–4**: manage predominantly to slow progression to ESRD

In 2012, Kidney Disease – Improving Global Outcomes (KDIGO) reconsidered the accepted classification given above and noted two clinically relevant deficiencies. The first was that there was no reference to the cause of CKD. This is clearly important in the clinical setting because the risk of progression to end-stage renal disease and the risk of cardiovascular complications differ for different renal diseases (diabetes versus polycystic kidney disease, for instance). Secondly, the binary risk of significant proteinuria being present or absent may be an over-simplification, as risk increases with greater amounts of proteinuria.

Accordingly, the KDIGO classification takes into account three factors when describing CKD and the risk it poses to a given individual: renal diagnosis, proteinuria and eGFR. The renal diagnosis is divided into seven categories, with an eighth miscellaneous group. These individuals are then stratified on the basis of eGFR into the same classes of CKD (stages 1–5, with the prefix G to denote GFR) as given earlier, but also into three additional classes according to the amount of albuminuria (A1–3, the prefix A denoting albuminuria). The classification is shown in Table 2.2. Examples of patients classified using this system, and how this might be used to guide risk stratification and management, are shown in Table 2.3.

Table 2.2 *KDIGO 2012 classification of CKD: individuals are classified according to diagnosis and then further stratified according to eGFR (G1–5) and albuminuria (A1–3).*

Cause of CKD	eGFR category (ml/min/1.73m2)		Albuminuria category (ACR, mg/mmol)	
Diabetes	G1	≥90	A1	<3
Hypertension	G2	60–89	A2	3–29
Glomerular	G3a	45–59	A3	≥30
Tubulointerstitial	G3b	30–44		
Vascular	G4	15–29		
Systemic disease	G5	<15		
Cystic and Congenital				
Other or unknown				

Table 2.3 *Clinical examples of CKD classified according to the KDIGO 2012 classification. Note from the comments how knowledge of the diagnosis, the degree of renal excretory impairment and the amount of proteinuria all contribute to an understanding of risk and how this might be managed.*

Cause	GFR category	Albuminuria category	Criterion for CKD	Comment
Diabetic kidney disease	G5	A3	Reduced GFR, albuminuria	Specialist pre-dialysis care
Polycystic kidney disease	G2	A1	Imaging abnormality	Most common single genetic mutation
Hypertensive kidney disease	G4	A2	Reduced GFR and albuminuria	Long-standing hypertension, refer (severely reduced GFR)
Reflux nephropathy	G1	A1	Imaging abnormality	Infrequent monitoring
CKD presumed due to DM & HT	G3a	A2	Reduced GFR and albuminuria	Very common, may not require referral
CKD cause unknown	G3b	A1	Reduced GFR	Common, may not require referral

The KDIGO classification is more descriptive of the problems facing an individual with CKD, and this may be important to those with a specialist interest in CKD. However, this has been achieved at the price of increased complexity, which may limit its usefulness in primary care.

Key points

- CKD cannot be diagnosed by a single abnormal eGFR result. The decrease in eGFR must be reproducible over more than three months.
- Proteinuria is as relevant to the diagnosis of CKD as a low eGFR. The patient has not been properly classified without some reference to it.
- The cause of CKD is important in determining risk. This is reflected in up-to-date classification systems.

References and further reading

Kidney Disease Improving Global Outcomes (KDIGO). (2012). Clinical Practice Guidelines.
www.kdigo.org/clinical_practice_guidelines

National Institute for Health and Clinical Excellence (NICE). (2008). Chronic kidney disease: Early identification and management in adults in primary and secondary care.
http://guidance.nice.org.uk/CG73

The Renal Association. (2011). Detection, Monitoring and Care of Patients with CKD.
www.renal.org/Clinical/GuidelinesSection/Detection-Monitoring-and-Care-of-Patients-with-CKD.aspx

3

Normal kidney function and what goes wrong in CKD

The kidney is a complex organ with a number of important functions. This complexity is somehow appealing to nephrologists (particularly those with a research interest), but has been a great disincentive for non-specialists to gain an understanding of kidney disease. For this reason, this chapter will describe the structure and function of the kidneys only as far as they relate to everyday clinical practice

Kidney size and shape in the diagnosis of renal disease

The kidneys lie in the loins (high in the posterior abdomen, adjacent to the vertebral column). The left kidney lies higher than the right kidney because of the presence of the right lobe of the liver. The kidneys are bean-shaped with smooth outlines, and they are usually around 10–12cm in length (see Figure 3.1). Renal size relates to the size of the individual, so 9cm-long kidneys may be normal for a small female but are definitely small for a tall male. For this reason it is not possible to give a clinically useful 'normal range' for renal size. Suffice to say that kidneys of 8cm or less in length are rarely normal.

Assessment of renal size by ultrasound is often desirable at an early stage when assessing patients with abnormal renal function. Renal shrinkage is a characteristic of CKD (although this may be absent in diabetic nephropathy and infiltrative disease such amyloidosis). Adult polycystic kidney disease is the one situation where CKD is associated with kidney enlargement; the finding of renal cysts usually makes this diagnosis obvious.

The renal shrinkage that usually occurs in CKD predominantly affects the cortex rather than the medulla. Specific mention of reduction of cortical thickness in the ultrasound report may therefore be helpful in confirming CKD when measurement of overall renal size gives an equivocal impression.

The common causes of CKD result in diffuse parenchymal disease, which causes a similar degree of shrinkage in both kidneys. When an ultrasound examination detects a disparity in renal size (a difference of 2cm or more), the implication is that each kidney is being affected differently by the disease process. Common causes of this appearance are renovascular disease and chronic pyelonephritis/reflux nephropathy.

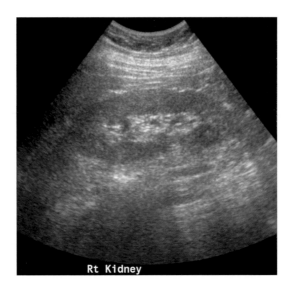

Figure 3.1 *Ultrasound examination of normal kidney. Note the smooth outline of the kidney. The darker outer area (cortex) contrasts in echogenicity with the brighter inner area (the medulla). The thickness of the cortex (normal in this picture) is easily measured and is useful in differentiating acute from chronic renal dysfunction.*

The outlines of the kidneys may be pitted or scarred by disease. In general, smooth outlines result from diffuse parenchymal disease (such as diabetic nephropathy, glomerulonephritis or hypertension), whereas scarring implies more episodic focal disease (such as chronic pyelonephritis/reflux nephropathy or ischaemia/infarction). Such scarring may be evident on ultrasound but is particularly well demonstrated by DMSA isotope scanning (see Figure 3.2).

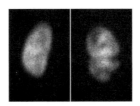

Figure 3.2 *DMSA isotope scan in a patient with reflux nephropathy. Scarred areas of the renal cortex take up less of the radio-isotope, leading to an uneven, mottled appearance. This is seen in the left kidney (shown in the right-hand image).*

Renal ultrasound is also the investigation of choice to demonstrate ureteric obstruction. It is therefore mandatory to undertake this investigation in any patient presenting with an abrupt loss of renal function. Table 3.1 summarises the interpretation of ultrasound findings.

Table 3.1 *Interpretation of renal ultrasound appearance in CKD. These findings need to be interpreted in the light of the other clinical features, as discussed fully in Chapter 8.*

Ultrasound appearance	Common causes
Normal-sized kidneys	Suggests acute rather than chronic kidney dysfunction (but renal size may be preserved in diabetic nephropathy)
Small, smooth kidneys	Hypertension; Chronic glomerulonephritis; Diabetic nephropathy
Small, scarred kidneys	Ischaemic nephropathy/embolic disease; Chronic pyelonephritis/reflux nephropathy
Asymmetric kidneys	Renovascular disease; Chronic pyelonephritis/reflux nephropathy; Long-standing structural damage (e.g. trauma)
Multiple cysts	Simple cysts; Polycystic kidney disease (see Chapter 8)

Clinically relevant pathophysiology of CKD

Glomerular function and glomerulosclerosis

Each kidney is made up of about 1 million nephrons bound together by interstitial tissue. Each nephron consists of a glomerulus (which is essentially a blood vessel tied in a knot) and a renal tubule. The glomerulus should be thought of as a filter, whereas the tubule orchestrates subsequent electrolyte and water handling.

Blood enters the glomerulus via the afferent arteriole and leaves via the efferent arteriole. Under hydrostatic pressure, plasma filters through tiny filtration slits between the endothelial cells (these cells are called podocytes) to enter the capsular space. The resulting filtered fluid (filtrate) then drains into the proximal convoluted tubule. The rate at which the kidneys can produce filtrate (glomerular filtration rate or GFR) depends on an adequate blood supply and the integrity of the glomerular capillary tuft – hence its clinical use as the measure of kidney health.

A total of 25% of cardiac output goes to the kidneys to take a first pass through the glomeruli. The kidneys are therefore very 'vascular' organs. This is what makes them so susceptible to diseases that affect vascular endothelium – most notably hypertension and diabetes but also rarer immune-mediated diseases. These conditions all affect the kidney by damaging the glomerulus and causing sclerosis (a Greek word meaning 'turning to glass'). In this process the blood vessels are replaced by deposits of amorphous collagen (fibrosis), which obstructs blood flow and stops filtration (see Figure 3.3).

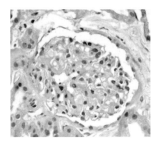

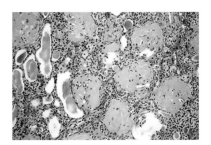

Figure 3.3a
A normal glomerulus.

Figure 3.3b *Glomerulosclerosis with obliteration of the capillaries. Blood can no longer flow through this glomerulus and filtration ceases. If glomerulosclerosis is widespread, progressive CKD may occur.*

Once the glomeruli are sclerosed, they never recover. As the sclerotic process progresses, the reduction in the number of functioning glomeruli is reflected in a decreasing GFR. In end-stage renal disease, the number of sclerosed glomeruli is so far reduced that the combined function of remaining glomeruli is insufficient to sustain health.

Whatever the cause, progression of glomerulosclerosis becomes self-perpetuating once the number of functioning glomeruli falls below a critical mass. This means that in advanced renal damage correcting the cause of CKD (say, hypertension) cannot stop the progress of glomerulosclerosis; it can only slow it down.

The mechanism by which glomerulosclerosis is thought to become self-perpetuating is illustrated in Figure 3.4. When a critical number of glomeruli are destroyed by glomerulosclerosis, renal excretory function is maintained by haemodynamic adaptations within the kidney. Under the influence of local hormones (e.g. prostaglandins) blood is shunted preferentially to those glomeruli with preserved function thus sustaining overall filtration capacity. But this increased blood flow causes hypertension in these glomeruli, which in time worsens vascular damage and accelerates glomerulosclerosis. This same process occurs regardless of the cause of the initial renal insult – whether it be longstanding hypertension or surgical removal of more than three-quarters of a patient's renal tissue for kidney cancer (leaving initially-healthy kidney tissue behind). Once a critical mass of renal tissue is lost, progressive glomerulosclerosis leads to failure of the rest.

An understanding of this process is clinically relevant. For instance, the mechanism whereby non-steroidal anti-inflammatory drugs (NSAIDs) temporarily worsen renal function in CKD is due to their effects on intra-renal prostaglandins. By interfering with production of these, NSAIDs inhibit the haemodynamic adaptations described above whereby blood is shunted to relatively-preserved glomeruli. Reduced perfusion of the healthiest glomeruli leads to a fall in

GFR and a tendency to salt and water retention. Another example of how these processes are clinically relevant is in understanding the renoprotective effect of angiotensin converting enzyme inhibitors and angiotensin receptor blockers (see Chapter 9). Unlike other anti-hypertensive drugs, the hypotensive effect of these agents is produced by specifically causing dilatation of the afferent glomerular blood vessel. In CKD this ameliorates the intraglomerular hypertension which is driving disease progression.

Whilst haemodynamic changes are central to progression of CKD, other mechanisms may also be relevant. CKD seems to engender a state of low-grade chronic inflammation and there is emerging evidence that this may contribute to the progressive nature of the disease. It is thought that the inflammation activates renal fibroblasts causing them to increase collagen deposition in the glomeruli, thus leading to progressive glomerulosclerosis. If this process is important, there is scope for developing pharmaceutical agents to disrupt these inflammatory pathways and to slow (or even reverse) CKD progression.

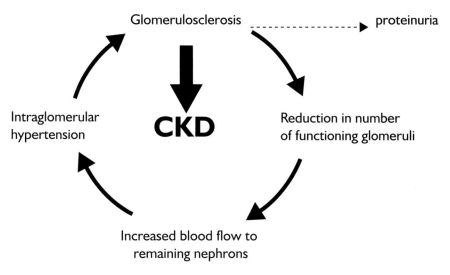

Figure 3.4 *Mechanism for progression of CKD: widespread glomerulosclerosis is the result of a self-perpetuating cycle in which a reduction in the number of functioning glomeruli places additional demands on those remaining, so leading to their accelerated sclerosis and failure.*

Tubular function and dysfunction

The filtrate (which is normally being produced by the glomeruli at a combined rate of around 100ml/ minute) is processed by the tubular epithelium to fully absorb essential nutrients (such as amino acids and glucose), absorb the required amount of each electrolyte (and excrete that which is not required), maintain acid-base homeostasis and reabsorb all but a small amount of water.

Two mechanisms facilitate this reabsorption of water into the circulation. The countercurrent concentrating system that operates in the loop of Henle (this mechanism is outside the scope of the present book) is quantitatively the most important. In the distal tubule and collecting ducts, fine-tuning of water homeostasis occurs under the influence of anti-diuretic hormone (ADH) produced by the posterior pituitary gland.

There is usually a degree of tubular dysfunction in advanced CKD. Evidence of tubular involvement includes chronic metabolic acidosis, hyper- (and sometimes hypo-) kalaemia and renal glycosuria. In CKD, the effects of loop diuretics (which interfere with urinary concentration in the loop of Henle – hence their name) may be severely attenuated. This is why nephrologists sometimes prescribe furosemide in doses as high as 500mg per day for CKD, in order to obtain a useful diuresis.

Usually, tubular damage accompanies or follows glomerulosclerosis. However, the extent of tubular functional impairment may occasionally be disproportionate to the degree of glomerular dysfunction (as measured by GFR). This situation can sometimes occur in conditions that cause predominantly tubulointerstitial damage (for example, the chronic interstitial nephritis that may accompany chronic pyelonephritis or myeloma kidney). As a result, some patients with CKD may present with nocturia, polyuria or postural hypotension. These symptoms occur as a result of failure of diurnal variation in urinary concentration or inadequate tubular salt reabsorption, which results from tubular malfunction.

The role of the kidneys in blood pressure control

Hypertension is a common cause of CKD, but it is also a common consequence of CKD because the kidneys are central to maintenance of normal blood pressure. There is therefore a 'chicken and egg' relationship between the two. Loss of blood pressure control in CKD may be caused by:

- Inappropriate salt and water retention as a result of reduced GFR and tubular malfunction.
- Over-production of renin (hyperreninaemia), which triggers excessive angiotensin/ aldosterone activity. This causes vasoconstriction, salt retention and excess ADH-induced water retention.

Salt and water retention causing hypertension is a feature of quite advanced CKD. Nonetheless, its importance as a contributing mechanism is illustrated by the effectiveness of loop diuretics to treat hypertension in this context.

Hyperreninaemia is the predominant mechanism for hypertension associated with reduced renal perfusion and is common in renovascular disease. In this condition, the up-regulation of renin levels required to maintain adequate renal perfusion (and thus filtration) causes systemic hypertension. This is clinically relevant because in this situation using drugs that block the effects of the renin/angiotensin system (angiotensin converting enzyme inhibitors or angiotensin receptor blockers) causes an abrupt reduction in renal perfusion and thus loss of renal excretory function (see renovascular disease in Chapter 8).

The kidneys as endocrine organs

Although usually thought of as excretory organs, the kidneys have an important endocrine role, particularly regarding anaemia and mineral homeostasis.

Erythropoietin

Erythropoietin is a circulating glycoprotein produced by cells in the renal cortex when they detect low oxygen concentrations in the blood. Hence erythropoietin is stimulated in response to anaemia, and instructs cells in the bone marrow to produce more oxygen-carrying red blood cells.

Failure of erythropoietin production occurs in advanced CKD (usually stage 4 or later) and causes anaemia. This hormone can be replaced with subcutaneous injection of a recombinant, as described in Chapter 11.

Vitamin D activation

Vitamin D must be hydroxylated in the kidney before becoming active. This vitamin has important functions at various sites around the body (including the immune system), but its major importance lies in its influence on calcium homeostasis. It is required for absorption of calcium from the gut and promotes calcium reabsorption by the renal tubule. It therefore has the net effect of raising blood levels of ionised calcium.

Failure of active vitamin D production in CKD causes a tendency to hypocalcaemia, which is compensated for by increased parathyroid activity, leading to chronic secondary hyperparathyroidism. This, in conjunction with phosphate retention caused by reduced filtration, leads to the bone disease and disseminated vascular calcification associated with long-standing advanced CKD. This is described in more depth in Chapter 11.

What happens in CKD?

Having understood the various effects of CKD on renal physiology, we can piece together how progressive renal impairment might manifest itself clinically. This can be summarised as follows:

Early CKD (stages 1–3b):

- Raised urea and creatinine levels in blood (reduced GFR)
- Signs of salt and water overload (reduced filtration, effect of renin) or, less commonly, depletion (tubular dysfunction and impaired urinary concentrating capacity)
- Hypertension (salt/water overload, hyperreninaemia)

More advanced CKD (stage 4):

- Hypocalcaemia, hyperparathyroidism, bone disease and vascular calcification (failure of vitamin D activation)
- Anaemia (failure of erythropoietin production)

Near end-stage CKD (stage 5):

- Acidosis (tubular dysfunction)
- Hyperkalaemia (reduced renal excretion and secondary effect of acidosis)

When unmodified by intervention, these elements finally come together to constitute the 'uraemic syndrome' of end-stage renal disease (see Chapter 17).

The non-specialist will probably not be involved in managing the effects of advanced CKD. However, knowledge of the pathogenesis and natural history of these effects is still useful. For instance, it is easier to appreciate the importance of blood pressure management in CKD if we know how glomerulosclerosis begins and progresses. Likewise, it is easier to understand why salt/water homeostasis and management may become complicated in moderate CKD if we know about the conflicting effects of impaired glomerular filtration and impaired tubular concentrating capacity. It is also easier to manage hypertension in CKD rationally if we understand the various factors that cause it in these circumstances.

The brief and intentionally-simplified account of pathophysiology given in this chapter provides all that a non-specialist requires to understand the mechanisms underlying CKD as it is encountered in clinical practice. Although my nephrology colleagues may be affronted by the superficiality with which this subject has been covered, further delving into the complexity of the cellular and molecular processes underlying CKD will now be left to them and their PhD students. As clinicians, we now need to develop our understanding of the benefits and limitations of tests used to identify CKD in the clinical environment. This will be the subject of the next two chapters.

Key points

- Renal shrinkage is typical of CKD and can be assessed by renal ultrasound.
- Renal asymmetry on ultrasound suggests renovascular disease or chronic pyelonephritis.
- CKD is caused by and also causes hypertension.
- Whilst hypertension and fluid overload are typical of CKD, disease affecting the interstitium more than the glomeruli may present with polyuria, hypotension and hypokalaemia.
- Advanced CKD is associated with bone disease, vascular calcification and anaemia due to failure of endocrine functions.

References and further reading

Meguid El Hahas, A. (2005). 'Mechanisms of Experimental and Clinical Renal Scarring' in *Oxford Textbook of Clinical Nephrology*. 3rd edition. (eds A.M. Davison, J. Stewart Cameron, J.P. Grunfeld et al.). 1647–1686. Oxford: Oxford University Press.

Shirley, D.G., Giovambattista, C. & Unwin, R.J. (2003). 'Renal Physiology' in *Comprehensive Clinical Nephrology*. 2nd edition. (eds R.J. Johnson & J. Feehally). 13–26. St Louis, Missouri, USA: Mosby, Elsevier.

4

Estimated GFR: Is it a good measure of renal function?

As outlined in the previous chapter, the kidneys have several metabolic and endocrine functions. However, in clinical practice, overall kidney health is conventionally described with reference to the glomerular filtration rate (GFR). Clinicians need a means of expressing GFR that is convenient and useful in everyday practice. The estimated GFR (eGFR) is now employed for this purpose. But what advantages does it have over other tests and what are its limitations?

Measured GFR

GFR can be measured in the nuclear physics department. This requires a marker (several molecules are in use) that is known to be removed from the blood exclusively by glomerular filtration. The marker is radionuclide-labelled and administered intravenously. By measuring the amount left in the blood at a known interval after the injection, its rate of elimination (and thus the GFR) can be calculated. The result, termed the 'normalised' GFR, is often corrected for body surface area (conventionally by expressing as 'per $1.73m^2$' which is the standard body surface area) and expressed as the 'corrected' GFR. This is the most accurate measure of renal excretory function that is widely available, but it is expensive, inconvenient and labour intensive to produce. It is not applicable to routine clinical use in the general population, although it is employed by specialists when they need to know renal function with great accuracy – for instance, when assessing potential kidney donors.

Surrogates for GFR

There are many metabolic waste products that are largely excreted by filtration through the glomerulus. It has long been appreciated that measuring the blood level of such substances might provide a useful surrogate measure for GFR. The ideal candidate for this role should be completely removed by glomerular filtration (in other words, there should be no excretion from the liver or gut) and should not be reabsorbed as it passes through the renal tubule. It also has to be measurable using a convenient, reliable and inexpensive biochemical assay. A substance meeting all these criteria has yet to be found. However, those currently in use are still clinically useful, provided the results are interpreted by a clinician who knows the clinical circumstances of the individual being tested and who understands the limitations of the test.

Urea

The first assay to enter widespread use as a marker of renal function was blood urea. It was noted that this was high in patients with renal failure – hence the term 'uraemia' for the associated clinical syndrome. In fact, it is not the urea itself that leads to illness and death, but the other unmeasured toxic products of metabolism that accumulate when the GFR falls.

Urea was measured simply because a convenient and reliable assay was available. However, it is not a particularly good surrogate marker for minor changes in GFR. It is produced by the liver during metabolism of dietary protein, so when protein intake is low or liver function is impaired, blood urea will fall, even when renal function is unchanged. Furthermore, when protein intake is increased (as might happen during gastrointestinal bleeding due to absorption of protein from digested blood) the blood urea will rise. Blood urea is also highly susceptible to changes in hydration status: in a dehydrated state, tubular reabsorption of urea increases, leading to an accentuated rise in blood urea. Urea often rises markedly during treatment with corticosteroids. Changes in blood urea may therefore not necessarily be proportional to changes in underlying GFR. A disproportionate rise in urea compared to creatinine is sometimes used as a pointer to a diagnosis of dehydration or occult gastrointestinal bleeding.

Creatinine

Measurement of serum creatinine concentration is used as a surrogate for GFR in everyday clinical practice. Creatinine is produced by skeletal muscle at a fairly uniform rate and is filtered from the blood by the glomerulus. Because muscle bulk does not change rapidly, changes in measured serum creatinine can reasonably be assumed to be due to renal excretory impairment. The test thus provides a convenient way to assess changes in renal function for a given individual. This is the best test when asking the question 'has this person's renal function changed since the last test?'

However, different individuals have different amounts of muscle. Clearly the rate of creatinine generation in a 25-year-old, 6-foot-tall muscle-bound rugby player is greater than that of an 84-year-old woman in a nursing home. Accordingly, recording a serum creatinine (which is a product of creatinine generation versus excretion) of 150mmol/l in these individuals indicates a minor deficit in GFR in the rugby player and significant renal failure in the elderly woman. A serum creatinine result therefore needs to be subjectively interpreted to take into account the build of the individual under investigation.

One way round this problem might be to measure the rate at which the kidneys remove creatinine from the blood and excrete it in the urine, as this would not be dependent on its rate of production by skeletal muscle. For this reason, the 'creatinine clearance' was used for many years as a special test for renal function. The creatinine clearance is not synonymous with GFR (some of the filtered creatinine is reabsorbed by the renal tubule) but the two terms are often confused with each other. Measuring creatinine clearance is inconvenient (it requires a 24-hour urine collection) and inaccurate in clinical use (timed collections usually are). It is therefore rarely used nowadays. It would clearly not be applicable to population screening initiatives.

Because of the influence of different creatinine production rates in different individuals, serum creatinine itself cannot reliably be used to determine a pathological lower limit of GFR in a population made up of people of different shapes, sizes, sexes and races. But many of the factors that affect the relationship between serum creatinine and GFR are known, so it should be possible to correct for these and derive a coefficient that is more applicable to screening for CKD. This is the idea behind formula-derived adaptations of GFR surrogates.

Formula-derived estimations of GFR

Formulae have long been used to adjust the serum creatinine to better reflect the underlying GFR. The principles behind these formulae are that (within certain limits):

- Muscle produces creatinine at a known rate.
- The amount of muscle correlates with weight and declines with age.
- Men have more muscle than women.

Accordingly, by measuring serum creatinine and then correcting for these variables, we can derive an estimated GFR. The validity of the formula can be assessed by correlating it with the isotope-measured GFR (the gold standard) in a sample population.

The Cockcroft-Gault equation was used in drug trials and clinical research for many years. But it was clinically limited by the need to include an individual's weight in the calculation. (This information is not routinely given on blood request forms or the adhesive addressograph labels used for identification.) A formula has been derived which uses empirical observations and does not require the patient's weight to estimate their GFR. With validation of this formula, the way was open to report eGFR from single blood samples using the patient information already available on the request form, and to use the eGFR as a comparator of renal function between individuals.

The 4-variable MDRD eGFR

The new formula took its name from an American study called 'The Management of Diet in Renal Disease (MDRD)', published in 1999. Because there were four inputs to the formula (serum creatinine, age, sex and a correction for race) it is known as the '4-variable' MDRD equation.

The formula was validated in individuals aged 18–75, with various degrees of renal impairment. (Note that these people had known renal impairment – the formula was not used to diagnose renal impairment.) There was a good correlation between the formula-derived GFR and the isotope-measured GFR, as can be seen in Figure 4.1. It should be noted that the correlation is greater at lower levels of renal function, whereas it is much looser in individuals with milder renal impairment. This is important, as we will see later.

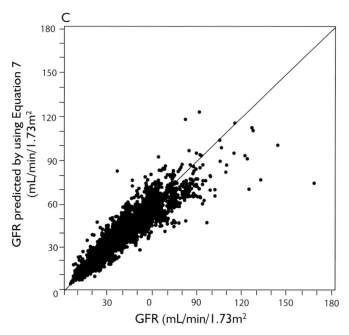

Figure 4.1 *The MDRD equation for eGFR. This graph shows the relationship between measured glomerular filtration rate (GFR) and GFR calculated using the MDRD equation for patients with various degrees of renal impairment. Note that the correlation between measured and estimated GFR is better at lower levels of renal function. (Source: M.S. MacGregor, 2007)*

Use of the 4-variable MDRD formula-derived eGFR was introduced to British medicine as part of the National Service Framework for Renal Services in 2005 and now appears on all laboratory reports when renal function is requested. It forms the basis of the classification of chronic kidney disease, which divides renal impairment into stages according to eGFR (see Chapter 2).

The adoption of the MDRD formula for universal laboratory-based estimation of GFR, and of the classification of CKD based on these estimates, has been controversial on several grounds. The formula is not perfect, and its use can result in misclassification of some people as having early stage 3 CKD, thus labelling them with a 'disease' where there may be none. The formula has not been well validated in the very old, or in ethnic minority groups other than African-Americans. Its use is not valid in children or pregnant women and it must be interpreted with caution in the following circumstances:

- In individuals at the extremes of BMI: The eGFR formula will overestimate true GFR in thin or emaciated people and underestimate it in those with high body mass index (BMI) or unusually high muscle bulk.

- In amputees: The reduction in muscle mass will reduce serum creatinine and lead to an overestimate of true GFR.

- In people with oedema or fluid overload: Here haemodilution of serum creatinine leads to the eGFR giving an overestimate of true GFR. In dehydrated people the opposite is true.

- In people who have had a high dietary intake of meat within the last 12 hours: Animal meat (particularly if stewed, as in goulash) contains a large amount of creatinine, which is absorbed into the blood after a meal and is measured by the serum creatinine assay. The eGFR will thus give an underestimate of true GFR.

- Prescription of trimethoprim: This interferes with tubular reabsorption of creatinine, leading to higher serum creatinine levels. The eGFR will therefore give an underestimate of true GFR.

These are predictable effects on eGFR results, which can be anticipated to allow the eGFR to be interpreted in the clinical context. Yet the QOF requirement to place all patients with an eGFR less than 60ml/min on a CKD register (without regard to clinical context) raises the possibility that some of these individuals are at risk of inappropriate management. One might reasonably argue that the eGFR was not intended (or validated) as a diagnostic test for kidney disease but as an improved substitute for serum creatinine in patients with known CKD.

Proponents of the wholesale introduction of the MDRD eGFR formula argue that, if doctors request a measurement of serum creatinine, they are doing so to acquire an estimate of kidney function, and the eGFR provides a much better estimate of this than serum creatinine alone. Furthermore, eGFR has been validated as a predictor of cardiovascular risk and of progressive CKD, so it is particularly useful in the individuals in whom it will largely be used (people with diabetes, hypertension and systemic vascular disease).

The prevailing opinion is that eGFR and the resulting CKD classification system will remain integral to international guidelines for the foreseeable future. Its advantages include simplicity of interpretation (estimated GFR approximates to percentage of normal kidney function), and the opportunities it provides for improved prevention of cardiovascular disease and reduced late referral of patients with established renal failure. However, these advantages only hold true if clinicians using the eGFR understand the limitations of the test – in particular, that it still makes assumptions about muscle mass and it has not been evaluated in all clinical circumstances. As we will see in subsequent chapters, this is particularly true in the elderly, where a low eGFR is a common finding.

MDRD vs CKD-EPI

The introduction of the MDRD eGFR formula to UK clinical practice in 2006 was an important if controversial change. It was a bold initiative to improve the rigour of CKD diagnosis with the intention of identifying patients at risk and improving their outcomes. However, because doubt remains about the utility of the MDRD formula in certain circumstances, other formulae are being evaluated which are likely to replace it in due course. The front-runner is the chronic kidney disease epidemiology collaboration (CKD-EPI) equation. Use of this formula results in higher estimates of GFR in young people, and lower estimates in the elderly. In routine clinical practice, where the population is predominantly elderly, this may lead to an increase in the number of people diagnosed with CKD and, of these, a higher proportion will be elderly. Can changing the mathematical formula used to manipulate the serum creatinine provide a robust distinction between health and disease? Time will tell, but there is little evidence to date.

Progress towards introduction of a new formula is likely to be slow because an international consensus is required for any changes to the current system. When a new formula is adopted, most clinicians will notice little difference – tests of renal function will still be reported as eGFR – but some patients currently on the margins of normality and some of those classified as CKD stage 3 may drop into or off the CKD register.

Cystatin C comes of age?

Cystatin C is a small 13kDa protein that is a member of the cysteine proteinase inhibitor family and is produced at a constant rate by all nucleated cells. Due to its small size, it is freely filtered by the glomerulus. It is then fully reabsorbed and broken down by the renal tubules without tubular secretion. The primary determinant of blood cystatin C levels is therefore the rate at which it is filtered at the glomerulus. This makes it a useful means of measuring GFR.

Unlike creatinine, cystatin C serum levels are virtually unaffected by age, muscle mass, gender and race. Several studies have found cystatin C to be more sensitive to actual changes in GFR in the early stages of CKD than creatinine-based eGFR. It is therefore considered to be a better test for the presence of significant CKD in the stage 3a range, when fluctuations in eGFR may cause patients to drift in and out of 'CKD'. It might also be more reliable for identifying CKD in the elderly.

Cystatin C assays have been available for over 25 years but their clinical uptake has been limited, largely because of the ease and ubiquity with which serum creatinine can be measured. However, as the shortcomings of creatinine-based formulae to estimate GFR have been identified, the use of cystatin C is now being re-examined. The KDIGO 2012 guidelines recommend that clinicians consider using cystatin C measurements in patients with CKD stage 3a (on eGFR testing) who do not have other evidence of renal disease.

Before cystatin C assays become widespread, there will need to be a population-based trial of its clinical utility and an evaluation of the economic impact of its adoption. These are in progress.

Where are we now?

Until these issues are fully resolved, it is vital that clinicians using eGFR do not simply equate a result persistently below 60ml/min with a diagnosis of CKD. The QOF may make this the criterion for entry on the CKD register, but as long as doubt exists about the application of eGFR to certain groups (especially the elderly) a clinically applicable diagnosis still requires proper evaluation for other signs of kidney disease and an attempt to establish a cause. Of the other manifestations of CKD, proteinuria is by far the most clinically useful and relevant – and this will be the subject of the next chapter.

Key points

- The most accurate way of measuring GFR is to use an isotope method. This is why it is used in evaluating potential kidney donors, where there is no margin for error.
- Serum creatinine remains a useful test for charting changes in renal function in a given individual.
- Estimated GFR is more accurate in advanced CKD than in marginal cases (stage 3).
- An eGFR less than 60ml/min is not a *diagnosis* of CKD – it is a valuable marker that should be interpreted in the light of knowledge of the clinical circumstances
- Cystatin C assays are likely to become more widely available in clinical practice and clinicians should be aware of the advantages of this test over eGFR in early CKD.

References and further reading

Coll, E., Botey, A., Alvarez, L. *et al.* (2000). Serum cystatin C as a new marker for noninvasive estimation of glomerular filtration rate and as a marker for early renal impairment. *American Journal of Kidney Disease.* **36** (1), 29–34.

Kidney Disease Improving Global Outcomes (KDIGO). (2012). Clinical Practice Guidelines. www.kdigo.org/clinical_practice_guidelines

Levey, A.S., Bosch, J.P., Lewis, J.B. *et al.* (1999). A more accurate method to estimate glomerular filtration rate from serum creatinine: a new prediction equation. Modification of Diet in Renal Disease Study Group. *Annals of Internal Medicine.* **130** (6), 461–70.

MacGregor, M.S. (2007). How common is early chronic kidney disease? A Background Paper prepared for the UK Consensus Conference on Early Chronic Kidney Disease. *Nephrology, Dialysis, Transplantation.* **22** (9), ix8–ix18.

National Institute for Health and Clinical Excellence (NICE). (2008). Chronic kidney disease: Early identification and management in adults in primary and secondary care. http://guidance.nice.org.uk/CG73

The Renal Association. (2011). Detection, Monitoring and Care of Patients with CKD. www.renal.org/Clinical/GuidelinesSection/Detection-Monitoring-and-Care-of-Patients-with-CKD.aspx

van den Brand, J.A., van Boekel, G.A., Willems, H.L. *et al.* (2011). Introduction of the CKD-EPI equation to estimate glomerular filtration rate in a Caucasian population. *Nephrology Dialysis Transplantation.* **26** (10), 3176–81.

5

Tests for Proteinuria:
What do they all mean?

Testing urine samples for the presence of proteinuria is an essential element in identifying CKD. It has been a key investigation since the original description of renal failure by Richard Bright in the nineteenth century. Detection of proteinuria is diagnostically useful (notably in diabetic nephropathy) but also allows stratification of risk in patients with renal disease, thus enabling therapeutic interventions to be appropriately targeted. For this reason, the detection of proteinuria in patients with CKD and appropriate subsequent intervention have been established as indicators in the Quality and Outcomes Framework (QOF).

Although the central importance of proteinuria is accepted, there are a number of issues relating to it that still cause controversy and can be confusing. These include the following questions:

- Which proteinuria tests should be used to screen people?
- Which tests are preferred for the quantification of proteinuria?
- What level of proteinuria is 'significant'?
- How should proteinuria be used to guide therapy to reduce risk of CKD progression?

Which proteinuria tests should be used to screen people?

Urine specimen collection

As 24-hour urine collections to quantify proteinuria are now obsolete (see below), all analysis for proteinuria should be performed on 'spot' urine samples. Ideally, the sample should be an early morning urine specimen (first urine of the day), as this will have been produced whilst the individual was asleep and will therefore not be affected by orthostasis (which can sometimes cause a minor increase in observed proteinuria). Of course, obtaining such a sample can be difficult in a busy GP practice, so urine taken at other times of the day can be used. Should analysis of this sample suggest that protein is present, the test can subsequently be repeated on an early morning sample to confirm the result.

The effect of orthostasis is increased with strenuous exercise, so it is important that this is avoided in the 72 hours prior to giving the urine sample. Exercise can also lead to minor haematuria. In addition, it is important to avoid testing the urine during a menstrual period, as this can lead to contamination of the urine with blood.

Urine should be collected in a container created especially for the purpose. Patients often favour the use of cleaned jam jars, but this practice is really unacceptable and should be discouraged. Plain (no preservative) specimen pots are not expensive. For urine being sent for protein biochemistry, the sample need not be refrigerated as long as it is analysed within 48 hours.

Urine reagent sticks

These sticks have been in common use for 50 years. They have the advantage of being inexpensive as well as allowing simultaneous detection of other constituents (notably blood and glucose) in a single test.

The test for proteinuria works on the principle that the reagent pad undergoes sequential colour changes, from green to blue, as more protein becomes bound to it. It is important to appreciate that different proteins bind to different extents. Albumin binds readily, whereas globulins and Bence-Jones proteins (indicative of myeloma) hardly bind at all. Consequently, the pad detecting proteinuria on the 'multistix' dipstick is really a test of urinary albumin, rather than total protein. These sticks can detect albumin at concentrations as low as 250mg/ml, although they are designed to become positive (+) at a protein concentration of 300mg/24hr. They are therefore not sufficient to detect microalbuminuria (defined later in this chapter). If microalbuminuria is to be detected, a stick designed for this specific purpose (such as Microalbustik™) must be used.

The degree of protein binding to the reagent pad is highly dependent on urine pH. Accordingly, false positive tests may occur when the urine is heavily alkalinised (as in patients treated with potassium citrate for dysuria). Because the sticks measure protein concentration, they are affected by the degree of hydration (which determines the concentration of the urine). It is therefore possible for concentrated urine (i.e. high specific gravity – another variable measured by the multi-reagent stick) to give a false positive result. Furthermore, false negatives may occur when the urinary protein is of a type not detected by the stick (such as paraproteins in myeloma).

The result of the dipstick is expressed in a semi-quantitative way (such as Negative, +, ++, +++). Whilst this is a useful guide, it is subject to observer error and bias. Automated devices that can read the colour changes of reagent strips using reflectance spectrometry reduce inter-operator variability and increase diagnostic accuracy.

Although reagent sticks may have a place as an initial screening test, they do not provide sufficiently accurate quantification to give a basis for therapeutic decisions. They are also hampered by the effect of urinary concentration. For this reason, quantitative laboratory methods are often used when more accurate quantification is required.

Which tests are preferred for the quantification of proteinuria?

In patients with a positive dipstick test, urinary protein excretion was traditionally assessed by means of a 24-hour urine collection. If accurately performed, this undoubtedly provided the most precise measurement of proteinuria. However, the clinical utility of 24-hour urine collections was limited by inconvenience to patients, inaccurate collections and the burden on laboratory staff having to process the specimens. For all these reasons, 24-hour urine collections have been replaced by more convenient methods on spot urine samples.

As noted earlier, the protein concentration in a spot urine sample is affected by hydration status. This problem may conveniently be overcome by relating the protein content of the urine to its creatinine content. The latter is produced at a fairly uniform rate, and changes in its urinary concentration are largely due to dilution. By comparing urinary creatinine concentration to protein concentration, a true measure of protein excretion can be obtained. This can be expressed as either the protein:creatinine ratio (PCR) or the albumin:creatinine ratio (ACR), depending whether all the protein in the urine is quantified or only the albumin.

Several studies have shown good correlations between ACR and PCR on early-morning spot urine sample and 24-hour urinary protein excretion. Furthermore, urine PCR has been shown to predict the risk of progression of CKD at least as reliably as 24-hour urinary protein excretion. ACR and PCR are now therefore the standard quantitative measures of urinary protein.

Both methods are derived by turbidimetric assays, in which the amount of protein is measured by evaluating the translucency of a sample after the proteins have precipitated, following denaturing by chemical means. Protein is difficult to measure in urine because the concentrations are low and subject to interference by non-protein substances. Also, different urinary proteins respond differently to the precipitation process. Accordingly, neither ACR nor PCR have emerged as clearly superior, and both remain in widespread clinical use. This is a source of confusion.

ACR or PCR?

ACR was originally introduced as a means of detecting microalbuminuria in people with diabetes. PCR originated in nephrology clinics as a way of monitoring patients with heavy proteinuria. Each measure remains the best for the task for which it was first introduced. However, studies aiming to establish the relationship between proteinuria and renal prognosis in CKD have used a variety of quantitative methods with no simple means of extrapolating from one to the other. This has led to debate about which of these measures should be adopted in general practice for guiding therapeutic interventions in CKD. Each measure has its advocates.

PCR measures all the protein in the urine. As urine may contain variable amounts of several different proteins, urine PCR will generally be higher than ACR by a variable amount. PCR bears a useful relationship to the 24-hour urinary protein (which also measures all the protein in the urine). If one assumes a daily creatinine excretion of 10mmol/day (which is about average for a physiologically normal male), the PCR expressed in mg/mmol is approximately the same as the number of grammes/24 hours of urinary protein excretion. This is convenient when one is used to working with the older measure – for instance, 'nephrotic-range' proteinuria, traditionally in the region of 5g/24hrs, can now be identified at a PCR of 500mg/mmol. However, it should be noted that the relationship between PCR and 24-hour protein does not hold true in patients with unusually large or small muscle mass. This is because the assumption that they produce 10mmol/day of creatinine is no longer accurate. There is no easy way of extrapolating between ACR and PCR or 24-hour urinary protein.

ACR measures only the albumin content of the urine. Its major advantage over PCR is its value in detecting microalbuminuria, which is known to be an important prognostic factor in people with diabetes. Detection of microalbuminuria is now embedded in clinical practice guidelines relating to both type 1 and type 2 diabetes, and its value in these circumstances is not contentious. As ACR is useful in diabetes, there is an argument that its use should be extended into the non-diabetic population, thereby obviating the need for PCR and removing any confusion that may arise from the existence of two tests. In fact, this is the view taken by NICE, who recommended that ACR should be the test of choice in CKD.

A major drawback is that albumin is more expensive to measure than total protein. The ACR assay is therefore approximately 2–3 times more expensive that PCR. One might question the value of detecting low-level proteinuria in the non-diabetic population when, according to current guidelines, this has no impact on management. Furthermore, there is some evidence that significant proteinuria can be missed if one relies entirely on urine ACR measurements.

The decision to measure PCR or ACR will depend on local factors, including cost and preference of local specialists. Notwithstanding this, NICE made a fairly unequivocal recommendation in the 2008 guidance:

- Do not use reagent strips to identify proteinuria (unless specifically designed to detect low-level albumin and express result as ACR).
- To *detect* proteinuria, use urine ACR in preference. (PCR may be used to monitor established kidney disease.)

This was followed up in March 2009 by a letter to all general practices from the Department of Health stating:

'NICE has recommended that to detect proteinuria the albumin:creatinine ratio (ACR) should be used in preference to other tests of proteinuria, including protein:creatinine ratio (PCR), 24hr collections for proteinuria and reagent strip ("dipstick") analysis'

This decision was based on the advantages shown in Table 5.1. The NICE document included a financial assessment, which concluded that screening for albuminuria in at-risk individuals using ACR was cost-effective, notwithstanding the additional cost of the assay.

Table 5.1 *The advantages and disadvantages of the proteinuria tests currently used in clinical practice.*

	PROS	**CONS**
Reagent strips	Inexpensive (less than 20p per test) Convenient, immediate Simultaneous screen for blood	Poor sensitivity for low-level proteinuria Measure protein concentration; quantitative interpretation thus affected by urine specific gravity Poor standardisation between manufacturers Operator-dependent
Protein:creatinine ratio (PCR)	Less expensive than ACR (£1–2 per test) Convenient relationship with 24-hour urinary protein excretion rate Strong evidence base of clinical relevance	Less reliable than ACR for microalbuminuria More inter-laboratory variation (compare ACR at low protein levels) Less convenient than reagent strips
Albumin:creatinine ratio (ACR)	Most sensitive test for albuminuria (predominant in low/moderate proteinuria) Readily standardised and reproducible Already established for diabetic renal disease Already incorporated into other international guidelines	Relatively expensive (£2–6 per test) Labour-intensive Questionable relevance to previous research Quantitative interpretation of heavy proteinuria uncertain

However, the NICE decision did not settle the debate. The Scottish Renal Association produced guidelines at the same time, Scottish Intercollegiate Guidelines Network (SIGN), and recommended use of the PCR rather than ACR, largely on the basis of cost. The Renal Association has recently produced guidelines that recommend use of either test. This apparent lack of clarity is the result of inconsistent interpretation of research data which is variable in quality, methodology and outcome, an effect which is further compounded by the degree to which different guideline authors take into account less 'scientific' aspects (such as cost and convenience) in their recommendations.

What level of proteinuria is 'significant'?

An important element in the PCR/ACR debate is how the level of proteinuria given by either of these tests affects therapeutic decisions. For instance, there is little point in favouring ACR because of its superior sensitivity if therapeutic intervention is first recommended at a level within the range readily detected by PCR. The key consideration therefore is to decide what constitutes 'significant proteinuria'. This task is made more difficult by the fact that different observational studies have used different means of quantifying proteinuria, and it is not easy to extrapolate between studies based on dipstick analysis and those based on ACR, PCR or 24-hour urine collections.

When timed 24-hour urine collection was considered the 'gold standard', less than 150mg protein/24hrs was considered normal, and greater than 300mg was considered pathological. Recent studies have used ACR, and there is consensus that ACR is an appropriate and sufficient test for quantification of proteinuria. An ACR of 2.5mg/mmol in men and 3.5mg/mmol in women approximately equates to 150mg protein/24hrs. Urinary albumin levels below this are considered normal. Table 5.2 shows the relationship between ACR, PCR and reagent stick in the diagnosis of microalbuminuria and macroalbuminuria.

Table 5.2 *How microalbuminuria and macroalbuminuria defined by urinary albumin:creatinine ratio (ACR) relate to urinary protein:creatinine ratio (PCR) and urinary analysis using a reagent stick.*

	ACR (mg/mmol)	PCR (mg/mmol)	Reagent stick
Normal	<2.5 (M) < 3.5 (F)	<15	
Microalbuminuria	2.5–30 (M) 3.5–30 (F)	15–50 (unreliable)	– or trace (unreliable)
Macroalbuminuria	>30	>50	+ or more

An ACR in the range 2.5–30mg/mmol defines microalbuminuria (roughly equating to a protein excretion of 150–500mg/24hrs). Neither the PCR nor standard dipsticks are sufficiently accurate to be used to detect or quantify proteinuria at this low level. The upper limit of the microalbuminuria range (ACR >30mg/mmol) is the level at which reagent strips become trace/+ positive and PCR becomes reliable – in other words, the proteinuria has entered the range traditionally regarded as 'clinically apparent' or macroalbuminuria. There is nothing particularly special about an ACR of >35mg/mmol in terms of risk to the patient. It's just that this is the level at which reagent sticks become positive and all the accumulated evidence relying on this measure can be used to guide management recommendations.

For patients with diabetes, it is clear that a urine ACR in the microalbuminuria range, as defined above, is 'significant'. The effect of microalbuminuria on risk and therapeutic decision-making in this context will be covered in depth in Chapter 14 (on renal disease in diabetes).

In people without diabetes, the evidence shows that proteinuria is a risk factor for CKD and cardiovascular disease, and the degree of risk increases in a continuum between normal urinary protein, through the microalbuminuric range and into frank proteinuria. This is true even in those patients with an eGFR greater than 60ml/min/1.73m^2. In one large study, the risk of developing end-stage renal disease in people with normal renal excretory function was 0.03/1000 patient years if there was no proteinuria, 0.05/1000 patient years if they had microalbuminuria (urinalysis trace or 1+, ACR 3.5–35 mg/mmol) and 1.0/1000 patient years if they had macroalbuminuria (urinalysis >1+, or ACR >35). In acknowledgement of this, most guidelines propose a series of thresholds of proteinuria at which a change in therapy will reduce risk. In the case of NICE, the thresholds are as outlined in Table 5.3. The 2012 KDIGO guidelines (see Table 6.1 in Chapter 6) grade risk according to low levels of proteinuria in the microalbuminuric range, even for individuals without diabetes.

Table 5.3 *How the presence and concentration of proteinuria affects management of patients with CKD, based on NICE 2008.*

NICE: Impact of proteinuria on management of non-diabetic CKD

- In patients without diabetes an ACR of <30mg/mmol (PCR<50mg/mmol) indicates *low risk* and does not require any specific intervention.

- In patients without diabetes, *significant* proteinuria is present when ACR is >30mg/mmol (PCR>50mg/mmol).

- Patients without diabetes who have significant proteinuria and hypertension should be offered angiotensin converting enzyme (ACE) inhibitors (or angiotensin receptor blockers).

- Patients with significant proteinuria in association with dipstick haematuria should be referred to a nephrologist.

- *Heavy* proteinuria is present when ACR is >70mg/mmol (PCR>100mg/mmol).

- Blood pressure targets in people with heavy proteinuria should be more stringent.

- Non-diabetic patients with heavy proteinuria should be referred to a nephrologist.

NICE recommends ACR as the screening method of choice and regards an ACR<30mg/mmol as conferring low risk. However, when ACR exceeds this level, PCR quantifies the proteinuria just as reliably. The stated advantage of ACR (that it is the most sensitive test for low-level proteinuria) therefore appears to confer little clinical benefit in the non-diabetic subject. It is largely because of this fine distinction between the two measures that both ACR and PCR are acceptable for the purposes of the Quality and Outcomes Framework (QOF).

Key points

- Testing urine for proteinuria is an essential element in assessing anyone at risk of CKD. No assessment of risk, or referral to a specialist, is complete without measuring the protein content of the urine.

- Either urine ACR or PCR can be used to quantify proteinuria; when low levels of proteinuria are present, ACR is more accurate; when it is heavier, PCR gives the advantage of correlating well with 24-hour urinary protein excretion.

- Both ACR and PCR are clinically useful and both are accepted by the QOF as evidence of adequate monitoring.

References and further reading

Brantsma, A.H., Bakker, S.J.L., Hillege, H.L. et al. (2008). Cardiovascular and renal outcome in subjects with K/DOQI stage 1-3 chronic kidney disease: the importance of urinary albumin excretion. *Nephrology Dialysis Transplantation*. **23** (12), 3851–58.

Caring for Australasians with Renal Impairment (CARI). (2004). Chronic kidney disease guidelines; urine protein as a diagnostic test. www.cari.org.au/ckd_urineprot_list_pub2004.php

Lamb, E.J., MacKenzie, F. & Stevens, P.E. (2009). How should proteinuria be detected and measured? *Annals of Clinical Biochemistry*. **46** (Pt 3), 205–17.

Levey, A.S., Eckardt, K.U., Tsukamoto, Y. *et al*. (2005). Definition and classification of chronic kidney disease: a position statement from Kidney Disease: Improving Global Outcomes (KDIGO). *Kidney International*. **67** (6), 2089–100.

National Institute for Health and Clinical Excellence (NICE). (2008). Chronic kidney disease: Early identification and management in adults in primary and secondary care. http://guidance.nice.org.uk/CG73

The Renal Association. (2011). Detection, monitoring and care of patients with CKD. www.renal.org/Clinical/GuidelinesSection/Detection-Monitoring-and-Care-of-Patients-with-CKD.aspx

Scottish Intercollegiate Guidelines Network (SIGN). (2008). Diagnosis and management of chronic kidney disease: A national clinical guideline. www.sign.ac.uk/guidelines/fulltext/103/index.html

6

CKD as a marker of cardiovascular risk

Observational studies of patients with a variety of systemic and kidney-specific diseases show that CKD is associated with a high risk of cardiovascular (CV) disease and adverse outcomes following CV events (see Figure 6.1). Such is the risk of CV disease in people with CKD that they are much more likely to die from the former than from end-stage kidney disease. Several studies show that a person at stage 3 CKD has approximately a 1% chance of reaching end-stage renal disease in five years, but a 25% chance of dying from CV disease.

The risk of CV disease increases as renal function worsens and/or the amount of proteinuria increases. The presence of combined renal impairment and proteinuria confers greater risk than either of these factors in isolation.

One way in which CKD might be associated with increased CV risk is via traditional risk factors. There is an increased incidence of hypertension, dyslipidaemia and diabetes in people with CKD, and the burden of these CV risk factors increases with the severity of kidney dysfunction. However, after correcting for these, most studies show that CKD confers its own independent CV risk. For this reason, screening for CKD (eGFR and urine analysis for protein) is now embedded in clinical practice as part of general CV risk assessment, and reducing this risk is an important aspect of managing CKD.

In advanced CKD, a situation associated with low-grade inflammation, vascular calcification and endothelial dysfunction, it is easy to envisage how CKD could have a direct effect on CV risk. None of these factors is relevant when CKD is in its earlier stages (when primary care teams are most involved in diagnosis and management), yet an independent association between CKD and CV events is still observed. This relationship remains unexplained, and this is why we must talk of an association between CKD and CV disease, rather than specifying cause and effect.

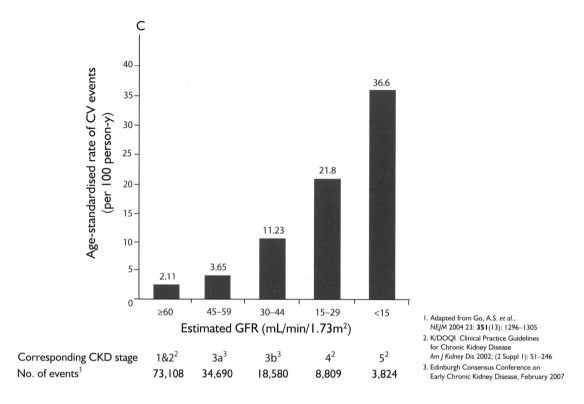

The following reference notes appear to the right of the chart:

1. Adapted from Go, A.S. *et al.*, *NEJM* 2004 23: **351**(13): 1296–1305
2. K/DOQI Clinical Practice Guidelines for Chronic Kidney Disease *Am J Kidney Dis* 2002; (2 Suppl 1): S1–246
3. Edinburgh Consensus Conference on Early Chronic Kidney Disease, February 2007

	≥60	45–59	30–44	15–29	<15
Corresponding CKD stage	1&2[2]	3a[3]	3b[3]	4[2]	5[2]
No. of events[1]	73,108	34,690	18,580	8,809	3,824

Figure 6.1 *The association between renal function (assessed by MDRD eGFR) and cardiovascular (CV) risk. A study of 1,120,295 adults within a large US integrated healthcare system showing how the risk of CV events increases as renal function declines. (Adapted from Go, A.S. et al. 2004)*

Assessment of cardiovascular risk in CKD

Although CKD (either low eGFR or proteinuria) has emerged as an independent risk factor for CV disease, it is not currently included in the CV risk assessment tools used in primary care, upon which reduction strategies are based. It is theoretically possible to adapt existing risk equations and normograms to increase their predictive accuracy, but adding yet another variable would be clinically cumbersome and has not been validated. There is thus an unmet need for new prediction equations that can be applied to patients with CKD. The 2012 KDIGO guidelines attempt to do this, but they have yet to be road-tested in clinical practice.

It is not sufficient to use merely the presence or absence of CKD to gauge an individual's CV risk. Since risk is affected by the severity of excretory dysfunction or proteinuria, this needs to be taken into account. CV risk is also affected by the aetiology of CKD via associated risk factors. For instance, an immune-mediated disease such as IgA nephropathy is likely to be associated with less CV risk than, say, diabetes or renovascular disease. This point underlies the emphasis placed by the 2012 KDIGO guidelines on the need to establish a diagnosis of CKD in order to fully assess future risk.

How can a clinician pull all these strands together to decide on appropriate risk factor management in individuals with CKD? The following is an attempt to answer this dilemma using an amalgam of research evidence and (where this is lacking) generally accepted expert opinion.

Hypertension

There is no robust trial-based evidence to show that blood pressure reduction in CKD reduces the risk of CV events because CKD patients are usually excluded from large trials examining the impact of blood pressure lowering on CV outcomes. However, since it is accepted that hypertension increases the rate of decline of renal excretory function in CKD, the increased CV risk attributable to CKD is coincidentally managed in this context.

In CKD, the recommended thresholds for anti-hypertensive treatment are lower than in patients without CKD, so one assumes that CV risk reduction will be a beneficial by-product of appropriate management of CKD itself. However, this is only an assumption. Management of hypertension in CKD is described in depth in Chapter 9.

Hyperlipidaemia

This is a contentious subject. Whilst it is accepted that both CKD and hyperlipidaemia add to CV risk, 2008 NICE guidance on CKD recommends that cholesterol reduction is only necessary as secondary prevention following a cardiovascular event. In other words, hyperlipidaemia in CKD is to be managed as in people without CKD. Whilst this seems counterintuitive given the additional risk burden carried by CKD patients, at the time this guidance was published, there was no epidemiological data to support a more aggressive approach.

However, in late 2010 the Study of Heart and Renal Protection (SHARP), the largest ever study of lipids and CV risk in CKD, reported its findings. This multicentre British study showed that lipid reduction at all stages of CKD, regardless of initial lipid levels, is associated with (on average) a 17% reduction in CV events. Large though the study was, it lacked a sufficient number of subjects to show a statistically significant reduction in all-cause mortality. Nonetheless, the authors concluded that all patients with CKD should be treated with statins regardless of their initial lipid profile. We wait to see if this recommendation enters CKD guidelines in future.

Proteinuria and eGFR

As described in Chapter 6, among patients with CKD observational studies have shown a graded increase in CV risk with the presence of overt proteinuria. The same is seen with eGFR<60ml/min. For instance, one study followed patients after a myocardial infarction and compared outcomes for those who had no evidence of renal disease with outcomes in patients with dipstick-positive proteinuria, low eGFR or both. Those with isolated proteinuria or a low GFR had a significantly higher risk of all-cause mortality (adjusted hazard ratio 1.7 and 1.4, respectively). The risk was greater in patients with both low GFR and proteinuria (adjusted hazard ratio 2.4). It would thus seem reasonable to take additional measures to reduce CV risk in people with proteinuria and low eGFR.

Once proteinuria is heavy (ACR>70mg/mmol, PCR>100mg/mmol), many authors agree that this should be considered a 'CHD risk equivalent'. In other words, the risk associated with this level of proteinuria confers similar risk as a previous CV event and thus warrants aggressive treatment in line with 'secondary' prevention. This is not enshrined in any current guidelines.

Risk reduction strategies in CKD

In established CKD, the most important intervention to reduce CV risk is rigorous blood pressure control as outlined in Chapter 9. There may be a role for lipid reduction, as described above, but this is not yet established in practice. Obviously, smoking and obesity should be discouraged in CKD as in other conditions. In patients with diabetic nephropathy, glycaemic control may be relevant to CV risk reduction (see Chapter 14).

The value of using antiplatelet agents to prevent CV events has not been studied in depth in CKD. There is a theoretical concern that aspirin may have a deleterious effect on renal function via its effect on renal prostaglandins (which are important for regulating intrarenal blood flow). In fact there is no evidence to support this concern and aspirin can safely be used, at a dose relevant to its antiplatelet effect, when required.

Current guidance

NICE guidelines for management of CKD have few specific recommendations relevant to CV risk reduction over and above the usual lifestyle interventions. The recommended blood pressure targets are predicated more upon their renoprotective effects than CV risk reduction (although the two are closely linked). Neither statins nor antiplatelet agents are recommended except for secondary prevention of CV events (in other words, the same as people without CKD).

However, the Joint British Societies (JBS) CV risk score (the usual method for calculating CV risk, which forms the basis for deciding if primary prevention is indicated) recommends that there is no purpose in calculating CV risk in patients with 'renal dysfunction' because they already have sufficient risk to warrant treatment with statins and antiplatelet agents. Whether 'renal dysfunction' is defined by low eGFR or proteinuria is not specified. It appears that differing interpretations of sparse evidence have led to inconsistent advice.

The 2012 KDIGO guidelines have used a meta-analysis of available studies to combine the major determinants of cardiovascular risk (eGFR and albuminuria) into 'heat maps' similar to the Sheffield Tables already in clinical use. An example is given in Table 6.1. Whether these diagrams come into routine clinical use remains to be seen, but the message is clear: the more advanced the patient's renal excretory impairment (see Table 6.1) and the heavier their proteinuria, the greater their cardiovascular risk and the greater the need for remedial measures.

Table 6.1 *Cardiovascular mortality determined by eGFR and ACR using pooled data from the CKD consortium. The relative risk (RR) is the risk incurred compared to normal: when RR = 1, the risk is the same as normal; when RR = 1.5 there is a 50% increased risk; when RR = 4 there is a four times increased risk, etc. (Data adapted from KDIGO Guideline 2012, courtesy of P. Stevens)*

	ACR< 1	ACR 1–3	ACR 3–30	ACR >30
eGFR >100				
eGFR 90–100				
eGFR 75–90				
eGFR 60–75				
eGFR 45–60				
eGFR 30–45				
eGFR 15–30				

Relative risk	
1–1.5	
1.5–2.2	
2.2–4.0	
>4	

Key points

- The presence of a low eGFR is an independent risk factor for future CV events.
- The presence of proteinuria is strongly associated with increased CV risk and augments the risk associated with a low eGFR.
- Blood pressure control is of paramount importance in reducing the risk of CV events in CKD patients.
- There is emerging evidence that lipid lowering and antiplatelet therapy are probably beneficial (and no evidence that they are harmful) in the context of CKD. Many nephrologists would recommend routine use of these agents in the presence of heavy proteinuria (ACR>70mg/mmol, PCR>100mg/mmol).

References and further reading

Go, A.S., Chertow, G.M., Fan, D. *et al.* (2004). Chronic kidney disease and the risks of death, cardiovascular events, and hospitalization. *New England Journal of Medicine.* **351** (13), 1296–305.

Keith, D.S., Nichols, G.A., Gullion, C.M. *et al.* (2004). Longitudinal follow-up and outcomes among a population with chronic kidney disease in a large managed care organization. *Archives of Internal Medicine.* **164** (6), 659–63.

Kidney Disease Improving Global Outcomes (KDIGO). (2012). Clinical practice guidelines. www.kdigo.org/clinical_practice_guidelines

Study of Heart and Renal Protection (SHARP). (2010). Randomized trial to assess the effects of lowering low-density lipoprotein cholesterol among 9,438 patients with chronic kidney disease. *American Heart Journal*. **160** (5), 785–94.

Tonelli, M., Wiebe, N., Culleton, B. *et al.* (2006). Chronic kidney disease and mortality risk: a systematic review. *Journal of the American Society of Nephrology*. **17** (7), 2034–47.

Tonelli, M., Jose, P., Curhan, G. et al. (2006). Proteinuria, impaired kidney function, and adverse outcomes in people with coronary disease: analysis of a previously conducted randomised trial. *British Medical Journal*. **332** (7555), 1426.

Wright, J. & Hutchison, A. (2009). Cardiovascular disease in patients with chronic kidney disease. *Vascular Health and Risk Management*. **5**, 713–22.

7

Kidney function in older people: CKD or benign decline?

To make rational choices in the management of patients with impaired renal function, it is important to appreciate that age is a major determinant of renal function and that the dividing line between healthy aged kidneys and true CKD is poorly defined. This chapter will help those dealing with elderly individuals to better understand the pitfalls of diagnosing CKD in older people, and how to judge therapy in each individual case to ensure the patient derives benefit.

How aging affects the kidneys

All the nephrons a human kidney will ever possess are fully formed by the thirtieth week in utero; there is no new development of nephrons after birth and there is no capacity for regeneration to replace those lost through damage or disease. There is great variation in the number with which an individual may be born, ranging between about 0.25 million to 1.8 million per kidney. In childhood, the number of nephrons in the kidneys remains fairly constant, but after 18 years of age there is a progressive decline in number – it is estimated that about 7000 nephrons 'drop out' per year. This loss has no demonstrable effect on renal function until about the fourth decade. Thereafter renal function declines progressively, with the GFR (note: the actual GFR, not the formula-derived eGFR) falling by about 1ml/min/year.

Aging is associated with a number of morphological changes within the kidneys which are thought to lead to this nephron drop-out. Study of this process has been hampered by the difficulty in separating the effects of co-morbidities (notably hypertension, atheroma and diabetes, which are common in the elderly) from changes that are due to aging itself. However, investigators have used animal models or transplanted human kidneys to minimise this problem and make some observations that may have clinical relevance.

Glomerulosclerosis was described in detail in Chapter 3 in the context of the pathophysiology of CKD. Even in the absence of known causes of CKD, the same process occurs as the kidneys age. This means that, by the age of 80, 30–40% of the glomeruli are totally sclerosed and non-functional. Non-sclerosed glomeruli show compensatory hypertrophy on histological examination of the kidney, presumably because of the demands placed upon them as other glomeruli fail. In addition to glomerular damage, the renal tubules progressively atrophy, causing loss of tubular function. This leads to impaired urinary concentrating ability and less renal resistance to hypoxic or toxic insult.

Renal blood flow declines after the age of 40. There is also a progressive increase in vascular resistance, so that less blood reaches the glomeruli for filtration. This process occurs in parallel with atherosclerotic damage to the larger vessels supplying the kidneys, which increases with age and further reduces renal perfusion

As a result of ischaemia, atrophy, sclerosis and fibrosis, the kidneys lose mass and it is usual for kidney measurements on ultrasound to show renal shrinkage in elderly subjects; the kidneys are similar in appearance to those with CKD. This raises an obvious question: is the loss of renal function seen in association with aging a disease or a normal phenomenon? Put another way, does finding a low GFR have the same health implications in the elderly as it does in younger subjects?

The effect of age on eGFR – the big debate

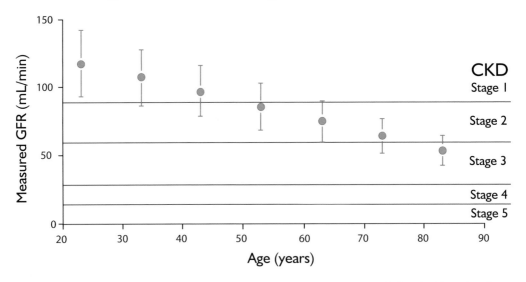

Figure 7.1 *Graph showing the normal range of GFR in the normal population at each decade. Note that the normal GFR declines with age. The horizontal lines represent the stages of CKD if the MDRD eGFR is assumed to be the same as the measured GFR. This places the majority of individuals over the age of 75 years in the category of CKD stage 3.*

Figure 7.1 represents the relationship between GFR (measured accurately by isotope methods) and age. This data is used when deciding if a potential kidney donor has sufficient renal function to donate half their renal mass and will come to no long-term harm if they do so. The implication is that these measurements are of 'normal' kidney function stratified by age and that the decline is not in any way pathological; there is still redundant kidney tissue that may be safely donated. In the graph, superimposed on the GFR ranges at each age, are the eGFR-based criteria for the various stages of CKD. It will be observed that there is an overlap between 'normal' renal function in some people over 70 (and most of those over 80) and CKD stage 3.

Although this decline in GFR (and by implication, eGFR) is accepted, the classification of CKD, and the treatment guidelines derived from it, take no account of age. According to NICE guidelines, the management of a 30-year-old and an 85-year-old, each with an eGFR of 50ml/min, is the same.

It might be argued that the MDRD formula includes a correction for age designed to take account of the age-related decline in renal function. But the validity of this in the elderly (those aged 75 years old or more) has not been established. It is currently the subject of ongoing research.

The formula for eGFR used in the MDRD study was validated in a population of Americans between the ages of 18 and 75, with varying degrees of renal function. As noted in Chapter 3, the relationship between eGFR and true renal function is less reliable when the degree of renal impairment is small. The formula is therefore least reliable at the tipping point between normal renal function and stage 3a CKD. As we saw in Figure 7.1, what is accepted as normal renal function in the very elderly (defined by GFR) is very close to the defined lower limit of normal renal function (age unspecified) by eGFR (i.e. eGFR<60ml/min). If there is an error in the eGFR that underestimates renal function in the elderly, a disproportionate number of otherwise healthy individuals will be defined as having CKD stage 3a.

Although CKD is currently defined using the MDRD formula, other formulae (notably the CKD-EPI formula mentioned in Chapter 4) change the numbers of individuals at each stage of CKD and attribute a diagnosis of CKD to relatively more individuals over 75 years of age. This illustrates the potential for misdiagnosis where renal function is on the margin of normality.

Since the introduction of eGFR measurement, there has been a great increase in the number of people diagnosed with CKD. It is estimated that just short of 10% of the general population have CKD stages 3a–5. It is also apparent that the majority of these individuals are elderly. In fact, in individuals over 85 years, CKD 3a–5 is more common than normal renal function (see Figure 7.2). In the absence of an upper age limit for entry onto primary care CKD registers, these elderly individuals are recorded as contributing to the so-called 'epidemic' of CKD and will presumably receive the same level of monitoring and treatment as their younger counterparts. But is this justified?

Even when a correction is made for co-morbidities, there appears to be a correlation between low eGFR and increased mortality. However, the impact of this effect decreases with increasing age (see Figure 7.3). Whilst some studies have failed to identify any relationship between mortality and eGFR in subjects over 75 years of age, others have shown that a significant adverse effect on outcomes first becomes measurable when the eGFR is below 45ml/min (CKD stage 3b or worse).

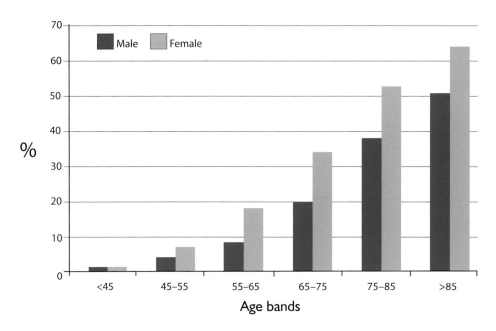

Figure 7.2 *The effect of age on the prevalence of CKD: the percentage of individuals in each 10-year age range diagnosed with CKD stage 3a–5 as defined by eGFR, subdivided by sex. (Adapted from de Lusignan et al. 2005)*

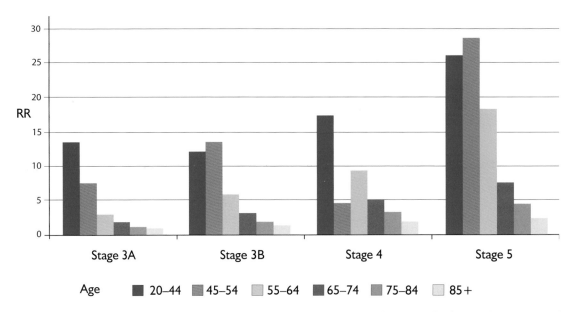

Figure 7.3 *Mortality risk (RR = relative risk compared to age match controls without CKD), stratified by age and stage of CKD. Note that the effect of CKD on mortality risk is dependent on age and is much less marked in older people. (Adapted from Raymond et al. 2007)*

If individuals over 75 years of age with stage 3a CKD are in fact at no increased risk of death compared to those with eGFR >60ml/min, this is important. Stage 3a–b CKD accounts for 56% of all cases of CKD, and of patients in this category about 65–70% are over 75 years old. Clearly, this will have a significant impact on currently recommended clinical practice. Interventions to reduce perceived but illusory risk are likely to do more harm than good.

In summary, the significance of an eGFR of 45–60ml/min in an individual over 75 years who is otherwise well, either as a diagnostic test or as a rationale for management, remains unsubstantiated. In this age group, evidence of an adverse effect on outcomes first becomes apparent at an eGFR less than 45ml/min and, even then, it is much less striking than in younger subjects. Clinicians must be fully aware of the limitations of the test and the implications of diagnosing CKD on the grounds of eGFR alone in older people. This is important because an inappropriate diagnosis of CKD is not entirely harmless: individuals may be caused unnecessary anxiety, may be financially disadvantaged (for example, with increased payments for holiday and life insurance) and may receive unnecessary treatment, which may in itself cause morbidity.

Many GPs have already made their own judgement about the significance of stage 3a CKD in elderly people. It is noteworthy that 40% of elderly patients on primary care CKD registers are unaware of their diagnosis. This implies that GPs attach so little importance to the diagnosis that they feel their patients are better off not knowing about it!

The correct approach when considering a diagnosis of CKD in elderly subjects is to make a clinical judgement as to the value of the eGFR result in each individual circumstance. The following factors may be relevant in guiding decision-making:

1. Proteinuria: It has been established that an ACR>30mg/mmol (PCR>50mg/mmol) identifies individuals at increased risk of mortality and adverse cardiovascular outcomes. Proteinuria is not a feature of the aging kidney. It can therefore reasonably be assumed that, regardless of age, the presence of proteinuria indicates significant risk and therefore provides a basis for intervention.

2. Subjective assessment of prognosis: Although it cannot be substantiated by research, most healthcare professionals can judge the difference between a 'good 80-year-old' and someone with a very limited prognosis. In aiming to reduce future risk, it makes sense to be more aggressive with risk management in those with longer life expectancies who stand to gain the most long-/medium-term benefit.

3. Views of the patient: To manage renal and vascular risk optimally requires several agents (see Chapters 6 and 9). Many older people may express a reluctance to take large quantities of drugs unless absolutely necessary. Given that the benefits of this treatment are less obvious than in younger individuals, it would be reasonable to give these wishes due emphasis.

Key points

- Renal function declines with age; the clinical significance of this is poorly defined by the available evidence.
- Using the accepted definition based on eGFR, CKD is present in about 65% of people over 85 years of age.
- The impact of CKD on the risk of cardiovascular events and all-cause mortality seems to be smaller in the very elderly. Management strategies, particularly where these include a heavy burden of medication, should reflect this appropriately.

References and further reading

de Lusignan, S., Chan, T., Stevens, P. et al. (2005). Identifying patients with chronic kidney disease from general practice computer records. *Family Practice*. **22** (3), 234–41.

Macias-Nunez, J.F. & Stewart-Cameron, J. (2005). 'The ageing kidney' in *Oxford Textbook of Clinical Nephrology*. 3rd edition (eds A.M. Davison, J. Stewart Cameron, J.P. Grunfeld et al.), 73–86. Oxford: Oxford University Press.

O'Hare, A.M., Bertenthal, D., Covinsky, K.E. et al. (2006). Mortality risk stratification in chronic kidney disease: one size fits all ages? *Journal of the American Society of Nephrology*. **17** (3), 846–53.

O'Hare, A.M., Choi, A.I., Bertenthal, D. et al. (2007). Age affects outcome in chronic kidney disease. *Journal of the American Society of Nephrology*. **18** (10), 2758–65.

Raymond, N.T., Zehnder, D., Smith, S.C.H. et al. (2007). Elevated relative mortality risk with mild-to-moderate chronic kidney disease decreases with age. *Nephrology Dialysis Transplantation*. **22** (11), 3214–20.

8

The first step in management: Establishing the cause of CKD

CKD is characterised by irreversible renal scarring. Down the microscope, we can observe the functioning elements of the kidney (glomeruli, tubules and intervening interstitial tissue) being replaced by fibrotic material as the condition progresses (see Chapter 3). Although nephrologists and pathologists draw a distinction between glomerular scarring (glomerulosclerosis) and scarring centred on the tubules (chronic tubulointerstitial damage), the two processes usually occur together. It is glomerulosclerosis that generally causes the gradual decline in GFR which is the clinical manifestation of CKD. Unless intervention can arrest the progression of glomerulosclerosis, it progresses to give the typical clinical characteristics of CKD:

- Progressive fall in renal excretory function (assessed by eGFR)
- Low-grade proteinuria (detected by urine PCR or ACR)
- Renal shrinkage (detected with renal ultrasound)

Once established, this process continues until the kidneys have insufficient filtration capacity to clear the blood of toxins. At this point, the symptoms and signs of the uraemic syndrome develop and the patient is said to be at end-stage renal failure. Table 8.1 shows the relative frequency of the major causes of CKD leading to commencement of dialysis in the UK.

Why establishing the cause is important

Since the advent of the Quality and Outcomes Framework (QOF) and the introduction of a register of patients with CKD, there has been an increasing tendency to regard CKD as a diagnosis in itself. However, simply detecting the presence of chronically reduced kidney function is not sufficient – some attempt should be made to establish why the renal disease has occurred. This is important for the following reasons:

- Potentially reversible causes of chronic renal dysfunction need to be excluded.

- A diagnosis gives prognostic information and guides management (aimed at slowing the decline of renal function).

- CKD can be one element of a more generalised condition that has manifestations at other sites in the body.

- A diagnosis informs family members about their risk of developing a similar condition.

- Knowing the diagnosis is important in those patients who may qualify for a transplant, as some primary renal diseases may recur in the transplanted kidney.

Because the risk of progression to end-stage, cardiovascular disease and other co-morbidities, differs between renal diseases, the 2012 KDIGO classification of CKD includes various diagnostic categories (see Chapter 2). Accordingly, this chapter describes the clinical features of the important causes of CKD and provides useful clues to aid diagnosis so that risk can be effectively stratified. Readers should note that **diabetes** is a common cause of CKD, presenting its own special diagnostic and managerial issues; it therefore has its own chapter (Chapter 14) and will not be discussed further here.

Table 8.1 *The percentage of patients starting dialysis with each of the primary diagnoses shown, given by age and male:female ratio (M:F). (Based on UK Renal Registry 2009 cohort)*

Diagnosis	All	Age <65	Age >65	M:F
Unknown*	20.7	15.0	26.6	1.8
Diabetes	25.3	27.3	23.2	1.5
Hypertension	6.9	6.0	7.9	2.0
Glomerulonephritis	11.5	16.0	6.9	2.2
Renal vascular disease	6.1	2.0	10.4	2.0
Chronic pyelonephritis	7.3	7.1	7.6	1.4
Polycystic disease	6.7	10.2	3.1	0.8
Other	15.5	16.5	14.4	1.4

* Includes presumed glomerulonephritis, not biopsied.

Hypertension

Because the kidney is instrumental in blood pressure control, hypertension is commonly associated with renal disease. This is unsurprising, since the final common pathway for progressive renal damage due to any cause is loss of functioning nephrons, leading to salt/water retention and/or hyperreninaemia, which in turn leads to hypertension. Clinically, the challenge is deciding if hypertension observed in a patient with CKD is the *cause* of the CKD or a *consequence* of it.

The true proportion of patients who develop CKD as a consequence of hypertensive glomerulosclerosis is not known. On the face of it, Table 8.1 above seems to suggest that hypertension is not a particularly common cause of CKD leading to renal failure. But these data must be interpreted with caution for two major reasons. Firstly, many cases described as 'cause unknown' have hypertension, but because a causative link cannot be proven (hypertension being so common in CKD, whatever its cause) they have been misclassified. Secondly, the classification system used to report the causes of CKD to the UK Renal Registry includes five different types of 'renal vascular disease' in addition to 'ischaemic renal disease'. In a clinical setting, these processes often occur together in a given individual, and it is difficult to disentangle which of them is the primary aetiology of the observed CKD. The recorded aetiology is therefore spread amongst a number of categories other than 'hypertension'.

Estimates of the prevalence of renal disease (as opposed to end-stage renal failure) as a consequence of hypertension vary widely and are also subject to reporting error. One large survey reported that 4% of all hypertensive patients have CKD, but this study was undertaken before routine reporting of eGFR.

The diagnosis of hypertensive nephrosclerosis is nearly always made on clinical grounds. On those occasions when a renal biopsy has been undertaken, the glomeruli show sclerosis, tubular atrophy and interstitial fibrosis associated with vascular hyalinisation (as seen in any other glomerular disease that causes glomerulosclerosis and, as a consequence, hypertension). Renal biopsy is therefore of little value in establishing hypertension as the cause of CKD.

In view of the close interrelationship between hypertension and renal disease, hypertensive individuals should be regularly screened for evidence of CKD. The diagnosis of hypertensive nephrosclerosis is likely if an individual with CKD has the following features:

- A history of long-standing hypertension (lasting several years)
- Low eGFR, reducing by <10% per annum
- Proteinuria may be absent but is usually at a low level (ACR<70mg/mmol or PCR<100mg/mmol)
- Dipstick negative for blood
- Small, unobstructed, equal-sized kidneys on ultrasound

The presence of significant proteinuria (PCR>100) or rapid decline in renal function (eGFR falling by >10% per annum) in a hypertensive individual is less suggestive of hypertensive nephrosclerosis, and another diagnosis should be considered.

Atherosclerotic renovascular disease (ARVD)

Atheromatosis is common. Outward manifestations of atheroma of the main renal arteries or the medium-sized arteries within the kidney are less obvious than in other organs such as the heart or brain. This is because humans are born with about five times more renal tissue than we need to survive, and this tissue is distributed between two kidneys. They can therefore soak up ischaemic and embolic damage. Only when repeated bilateral infarction leads to a critical loss of renal mass will the condition become overt. Ischaemic damage to the kidneys is common and may account for about 20% of cases of end-stage renal failure in patients over the age of 60. ARVD is commonly associated with vascular disease at other sites (see Table 8.2). As these manifestations of vascular disease are usually easier to identify clinically than ARVD, they can provide a clue to the presence of the latter.

Table 8.2 *The percentage of patients with vascular diseases who also have clinically unapparent, significant ARVD: a summary of the literature*

Vascular co-morbidities	Percentage who also have ARVD
Peripheral vascular disease	42%
Abdominal aortic aneurism	38%
Congestive cardiac failure	33.4%
Coronary heart disease	15%
Cerebrovascular accident	10.4%

The renal damage in ARVD is largely caused by cholesterol embolisation of the kidneys, leading to ischaemia and infarction. Additional damage is caused by the haemodynamic effect of reduced blood flow distal to the arterial stenosis. This causes reduced intraglomerular pressure in the affected kidney and activation of the renin-angiotensin system. The latter causes systemic hypertension and progressive hypertension-mediated nephrosclerosis in the contralateral kidney. When both kidneys are involved in this disease process, it becomes clinically manifested as irreversible CKD and is sometimes called 'ischaemic nephropathy'. End-stage disease may develop gradually by progressive glomerulosclerosis, or by a series of downward steps in renal function as segments of the kidneys are infarcted by thrombus or atheromatous debris. If a large thrombus or atheromatous plaque occludes the artery to the one remaining functioning kidney, patients may present with acute, anuric renal failure. The appearance of kidneys affected by ARVD is shown in Figure 8.1.

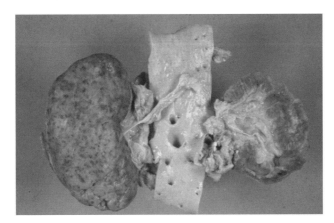

Figure 8.1 *This photograph shows the post-mortem appearance of kidneys from a patient with atheromatous renovascular disease. Note the mottled, irregular appearance of the renal cortices. This is caused by multiple small vessel embolic events. Both kidneys are shrunken, particularly the one on the right of the picture. Such renal asymmetry is typical of renovascular disease. (Photograph courtesy of Dr P. Kalra)*

There are two important reasons to consider ARVD when assessing a patient with newly identified CKD:

1. The effect of angiotensin converting enzyme inhibitors (ACE-Is): Because renovascular atheroma reduces renal perfusion, the renin/angiotensin system is up-regulated to maintain glomerular pressure. The introduction of ACE-Is or angiotensin receptor blockers (ARBs) interferes with this compensatory mechanism. The result is an abrupt reduction in renal perfusion and thus an acute deterioration in renal function. Whilst this is usually reversible on stopping the drug, this is not always the case and some permanent loss of function due to ischaemia may occur. (For more on this issue, see the management of hypertension in CKD in Chapter 9.)

2. Flash pulmonary oedema: The abrupt onset of severe shortness of breath with orthopnoea and paroxysmal nocturnal dyspnoea often mimics acute congestive cardiac failure and may lead to inappropriate management.

The clinical diagnosis of ARVD should be suspected in patients with the following features:

- Hypertension (often resistant to treatment)
- Impaired renal function, sometimes declining in a stepwise manner
- Proteinuria; usually (but not always) sub-nephrotic
- Atheroma at other sites (peripheral vascular disease, cerebrovascular disease, IHD)
- Risk factors for vascular disease (diabetes, hyperlipidaemia, smoking)
- Flash pulmonary oedema (especially if an echocardiogram shows adequate left ventricular function)
- Abrupt reduction in renal function after starting an ACE-I or ARB
- Renal asymmetry (>2cm) on ultrasound

53

Obstructive uropathy

This condition is important because it is a preventable cause of CKD. Patients with obstructive uropathy usually have bladder outflow obstruction and this is usually due to prostatic enlargement. Relief of the obstruction, if effected in time, can prevent continued renal damage and end-stage disease. Less commonly, bilateral ureteric involvement in pelvic disease (notably prostatic or cervical carcinoma) may cause obstructive uropathy in the absence of bladder outflow obstruction.

Usually, patients with prostatic disease will give a history of bladder outflow problems, but this is not always so. It is therefore mandatory to examine the bladder in elderly men presenting with CKD. If obstructive uropathy is considered a possibility, a renal ultrasound should be undertaken.

Obstructive uropathy should be considered in patients with the following characteristics:

- Elderly male
- Often a rapid deterioration in function
- Normal urinalysis or minimal proteinuria
- Symptoms of bladder outflow obstruction (but not invariably)
- Palpable bladder
- Obstruction on renal ultrasound

Reflux nephropathy/Chronic pyelonephritis

This condition is declining in incidence due to improved screening of children who are at high risk. It nonetheless accounts for about 10% of patients currently on dialysis.

Urinary infection usually causes cystitis or pyelonephritis. It is very unusual for these to cause lasting renal damage. However, in patients with structural abnormalities of the renal tract, the infection can persist and cause chronic damage. This is most commonly due to congenital incompetence of the vesicoureteric valves, whereby bladder contraction causes urine to reflux up to the kidneys rather than go out through the urethra. Stagnant urine harbouring infection can thereby persist within the renal tract. Over many years, the reflux of infected urine into the kidneys causes chronic interstitial damage and renal impairment. Because reflux and pyelonephritis are both implicated in the pathogenesis of this condition, they are both applied to its name.

The hallmark of reflux nephropathy/chronic pyelonephritis is renal cortical scarring. This can often be seen on ultrasound, but the most sensitive test is a DMSA renogram (see Figure 3.2 in Chapter 3), which also assesses the proportion of overall renal function contributed by each kidney.

The characteristics of patients with CKD due to reflux nephropathy/chronic pyelonephritis are:

- Middle-aged patient (often female, but not exclusively so), with past history of recurrent urinary tract infections or enuresis
- Sometimes a family history of recurrent urinary sepsis or kidney failure

- Proteinuria (usually PCR<300mg/mmol)

- Hypertension

- Cortical scarring and asymmetry of the kidneys on renal ultrasound or DMSA scan

Chronic glomerulonephritis

It is important to emphasise the distinction between acute and chronic glomerulonephritis. Acute glomerulonephritis is a nephrological emergency. Any patient presenting with:

- Rapidly progressive renal excretory failure

- Usually hypertension and fluid overload

- Systemic symptoms (anorexia, malaise)

- Microscopic or macroscopic haematuria

- Proteinuria (PCR>100mg/mmol)

should be referred for urgent (same day) assessment by a nephrologist (by telephone). They may require urgent immunosuppression to salvage kidney function. Management of acute nephritis is outwith the remit of this book on CKD. The important message is that speedy referral is mandatory; what renal function is lost to acute immune-mediated attack may be lost forever and the chance to avoid end-stage renal failure may be missed in a matter of days.

However, some forms of glomerulonephritis are more indolent and present with nothing more alarming than clinically quiet chronic renal impairment. The clinical features of chronic glomerulonephritis depend on the histological type but an abnormal urinary sediment is invariable. In early disease, a renal biopsy will establish the diagnosis and give an indication as to whether the condition is amenable to disease-altering treatment. In later disease, the biopsy shows non-specific chronic changes (glomerulosclerosis, as described in Chapter 3) rather than distinct histological patterns, and differentiation from hypertensive nephropathy becomes difficult. Accordingly, early referral to a nephrologist is very important.

It is important that the non-specialist does not become bogged down in the detail of various sorts of glomerulonephritides. It is as well to have merely heard their names and know that they exist and the syndromes they can produce. The most common histological types of chronic glomerulonephritis that can present with slowly progressive CKD are:

- IgA nephropathy: Often causes persistent microscopic haematuria or episodic macroscopic haematuria in association with intercurrent illnesses. Hypertension is frequently present. Progressive CKD occurs in about 20%.

- Membranous glomerulonephritis: Usually presents with persistent proteinuria, frequently of nephrotic proportions (PCR>300mg/mmol). In elderly patients, it may be a manifestation of occult malignancy. About 30% develop progressive CKD.

- Focal segmental glomerulosclerosis (FSGS): Presents with persistent proteinuria (often nephrotic syndrome) and progressive CKD (in about 50% of patients).
- Mesangiocapillary glomerulonephritis: Presents with persistent proteinuria (sometimes nephritic syndrome), microscopic haematuria, hypertension and progressive CKD.

Features that would favour a diagnosis of chronic glomerulonephritis in a patient with newly diagnosed CKD include:

- Hypertension
- Active urinary sediment (either proteinuria or microscopic haematuria)
- Urine ACR>70mg/mmol, PCR>100mg/mmol, sometimes much more
- Past history of abnormal urinalysis (as undertaken during a medical examination for the armed services or for life insurance).

Adult polycystic kidney disease

Adult polycystic kidney disease (APKD) is a multi-system disease characterised by multiple bilateral renal cysts in association with cysts in other organs such as the liver, pancreas and arachnoid membranes. There is an increased risk of subarachnoid haemorrhage, mitral valve prolapse and hernias. It is one of the most common genetic diseases in Caucasians, being present in about 1 in 20,000 live births.

It is inherited by 50% of the offspring of an affected individual (autosomal dominant inheritance). New cases are therefore often detected during a screening ultrasound of a member of an affected family. The cysts will be present by young adulthood in affected individuals. Only if they remain cyst-free at the age of 30 years can the diagnosis be confidently excluded. Those family members that are not affected have no increased risk of passing the abnormality on to offspring. Indeed, they should be treated as entirely normal – including being considered as possible kidney donors to affected siblings.

Although most patients have a significant family history, this is not invariably so. Unforeseen cases may be identified during routine investigation for CKD or hypertension. These cases arise from new spontaneous mutations or where paternity is uncertain.

Occasional diagnostic confusion arises when a patient with no known family history of APKD presents with a few renal cysts (which are common). By convention, to qualify for a diagnosis of APKD, an individual with a known family history must have at least three cysts and they must be bilateral. When no family history exists, they must have at least ten cysts in each kidney. The kidneys are usually enlarged overall. Chromosome analysis for the genetic traits of APKD is possible where doubt persists, but the diagnosis is usually made on the basis of clinical features.

All patients with APKD should be referred to a nephrologist for counselling and evaluation, but it is not necessary for them to be retained for regular follow-up. All that is required is regular monitoring of blood pressure and renal function, which can be done in a primary care setting. Whilst renal function is normal, hypertension should be treated as in any other individual. If renal function becomes abnormal, hypertension targets are those described in the current NICE guidelines for managing CKD (see Chapter 9).

There is some debate as to whether or not the offspring of an affected individual should be screened with an ultrasound, particularly since the condition is incurable. On the one hand, they stand to incur additional insurance weighting and perhaps discrimination in employment. On the other hand, early diagnosis allows regular monitoring of blood pressure and gives the individual useful information about what the future holds. This may be useful when planning a career and other aspects of life. There is no guidance for GPs to help them decide about screening. It is best to discuss the issue with the affected family and do what they feel is appropriate.

Because patients with APKD are at risk of subarachnoid haemorrhage (SAH) from cerebral aneurysms, the question arises as to whether or not APKD patients should be routinely referred for cerebral imaging (MR or CT angiogram) with the intention of prophylactically clipping any aneurysms that may be found. Opinion is divided because: (i) most aneurysms do not rupture; (ii) surgical clipping is risky; and (iii) one cannot be reassured that, because there is no aneurysm on a scan, an aneurysm will not develop in future. This is a difficult area and specialist advice should be sought.

However, there is general agreement on some issues:

- The risk of SAH is minimal before the age of 30, so screening prior to this date is not indicated.
- The risk of SAH runs in families; accordingly, people with APKD and a family history of SAH should be offered screening. The prognosis of people with large aneurysms, even when asymptomatic, is improved by prophylactic clipping.
- In people with a family history but no aneurysm on initial screening, repeat MRI should be undertaken roughly every five years.

People with APKD are often asymptomatic, but some patients complain of abdominal fullness (often as a result of liver rather than kidney cysts), loin pain and haematuria. Sometimes the haematuria can be concerning, particularly if it continues for days. In this instance, simple measures to stop the bleeding (such as bed rest and stopping aspirin) should be advised and the patient should be reassured that bleeding very rarely continues for more than seven days. It may be necessary to check the haemoglobin level if the bleeding is protracted, and the renal unit should be consulted if the patient is found to be anaemic. It is exceedingly rare for radiological intervention, to embolise the bleeding point, to be required.

The natural history of APKD is highly variable, but tends to run in families. An affected individual can therefore get some idea of what the future holds by observing the natural history of disease in a parent. End-stage renal disease typically occurs by the sixth decade, and renal transplantation is the treatment of choice at this point. However, end-stage renal failure is not inevitable. Studies have shown that as many as 60% of affected individuals are alive without end-stage renal disease at the age of 70; and it is certainly the case that some people with APKD die in their late eighties from an unrelated illness without their renal condition ever impacting on their health.

Other conditions

There are, of course, many other conditions that can give rise to CKD but it is outside the scope of this short book to account for them all. The great majority of patients encountered in primary care with CKD will have one of the conditions outlined above. You will see from the descriptions of each renal disease that they can be differentiated by undertaking the 'Five simple tasks' in Table 8.3 below. Where doubt exists regarding the diagnosis of the cause of CKD, referral to a nephrologist is advised. It is important to include in the referral letter the information outlined in Table 8.3.

Table 8.3 *Five simple tasks to undertake in any patient presenting with renal impairment. These should provide all the information required to exclude serious acute renal disease (requiring urgent referral) and will help establish the cause of CKD.*

Task 1:	Drug review: Has the patient started an NSAID, ACE-I or ARB?
Task 2:	Review of co-morbidities: Do they have a history of hypertension or diabetes? Are there features suggestive of widespread atheroma?
Task 3:	Urinalysis: Do they have significant proteinuria or haematuria?
Task 4:	Renal ultrasound: If they have frank haematuria, pain or urinary outflow problems or if you suspect ARVD.
Task 5:	Surveillance: Has their renal function changed recently? How fast is it deteriorating?

Key points

- It is not sufficient to diagnose CKD without looking for a cause.
- The cause of CKD affects management and prognosis – hence its inclusion in modern CKD classifications.
- In the majority of cases of CKD, a cause can be established by undertaking the five simple tasks in Table 8.3.

References and further reading

Caskey, F., Dawnay, A., Farrington, K. *et al.* (2011). UK Renal Registry 2010: 13th Annual Report of the Renal Registry. *Nephron Clinical Practice.* **119** (2).

Cassidy, M. & Ter Wee, P.M. (2005). 'Assessment and initial management of the patient with failing renal function' in *Oxford Textbook of Clinical Nephrology.* 3rd edition. (eds A.M. Davison, J. Stewart Cameron, J.P. Grunfeld *et al.*). 1687–1716. Oxford: Oxford University Press.

Conlon, P., O'Riordan, E. & Kalra, P.A. (2000). New insights into the epidemiologic and clinical manifestations of atherosclerotic renovascular disease. *American Journal of Kidney Disease.* **35** (4), 573–87.

Winearls, C.G. (2003). 'Clinical evaluation and manifestations of chronic renal failure' in *Comprehensive Clinical Nephrology.* 2nd edition. (eds R.J. Johnson & J. Feehally). 857–72. St Louis, Missouri: Mosby, Elsevier.

9

Preventing progression of CKD: Hypertension and ACE-inhibitors

Patients under surveillance for CKD stage 3–5 may have stable renal function for many years, or they may show slow decline as described in Chapter 3. It is important to understand that even exemplary treatment may not halt decline of renal function in CKD. An eGFR decline of about 1ml/min per annum is considered to be in keeping with the effect of normal aging. The original study validating the MDRD eGFR formula showed that adults with CKD progress at a rate of 2–5ml/min. This rate of decline is acceptable in a patient with CKD, providing the clinician is reassured that all remediable factors have been addressed.

NICE included in its 2008 guidance on management of CKD the following recommendation for identifying progressive disease:

- Obtain a minimum of three GFR estimations over a period of not less than 90 days.
- In people with a new finding of reduced eGFR, repeat the eGFR within two weeks to exclude causes of acute deterioration of GFR.
- Define progression as a decline in eGFR of more than 5ml/min within one year, or more than 10ml/min within five years.
- If such a decline is observed, referral for specialist advice should be considered.

This recommendation is a safeguard designed to improve detection of people with potentially treatable primary renal disease. Note that a 5ml/min change in eGFR is the same as the biological variation of the eGFR test, so more than one test will be required to distinguish people with deteriorating CKD from those whose eGFR is fluctuating for other spurious reasons (such as hydration or diet, see Chapter 10). Observing the trajectory of renal decline over months or years is key to identifying individuals at risk of developing end-stage CKD within their natural lifespan.

The main reason for identifying CKD early in at-risk individuals is to slow the rate of progression as far as possible, thus reducing the number of people reaching end-stage CKD. This chapter describes the measures that should be taken to achieve this – namely blood pressure control and the use of drugs affecting the renin-angiotensin system.

Blood pressure (BP) control: The cornerstone of CKD management

Effective management of hypertension in CKD slows progression towards end-stage renal failure. Furthermore, meticulous control of blood pressure is required to counter the increased risk of cardiovascular events in patients with CKD. However, such management also imparts special challenges: blood pressure targets are generally lower in patients with CKD, and the choice of drugs may be different from regimes designed for patients without CKD.

Before embarking on drug treatment of hypertension in CKD patients, each individual needs clinical assessment to establish whether medication is warranted and, if so, what first-line agent is most appropriate. The clinician should ask the following key questions:

- Does the patient have proteinuria?
- Do they have salt/water retention?
- Are they likely to have occult renovascular disease?
- Are they very elderly?

The influence of proteinuria on BP management

An assessment of proteinuria determines the choice of drugs and the target blood pressure. It also identifies those patients with heavy proteinuria who have primary renal disease and secondary hypertension. The quantification of proteinuria is undertaken using PCR or ACR, one of which is mandatory when managing hypertension in CKD.

In both diabetic and non-diabetic CKD, a statistically significant reduction in the rate of decline of renal function has been observed when angiotensin converting enzyme-inhibitors (ACE-Is) are used to control blood pressure in those patients who have proteinuria above 0.5g/day. Where proteinuria is not present, ACE-Is confer no benefit over other classes of anti-hypertensive agent, provided the blood pressure is controlled to the same extent. ACE-Is have no benefit on all-cause mortality unless patients are treated at the maximum tolerable dose.

The effects on mortality and CKD progression of angiotensin receptor blockers (ARBs) are similar to those of ACE-Is. Three studies have directly compared the effects of ARBs and ACE-Is and have shown no difference in their effects on mortality or renal outcomes. There appears to be no additional advantage to using a combination of ACE-I and ARB on CKD progression (although the combination is sometimes used, under specialist supervision, to control heavy proteinuria).

In the light of this evidence, the 2008 NICE guidelines on management of CKD recommend that, in the presence of proteinuria (defined as ACR>30mg/mmol in this document), hypertension should be managed first line with ACE-Is or ARBs. The dosage used should be titrated up to the maximum before another agent is added.

The influence of salt/water retention on BP management

Reduction of excretory function and abnormal salt/water handling often leads to fluid retention in patients with CKD, and can contribute to the development of hypertension. Where this is the case, correcting fluid balance may help in the control of blood pressure. Identification and correction of fluid retention should be an early intervention in patients with CKD and hypertension. Fluid retention is suggested by hypertension in association with:

- Pitting ankle oedema
- Shortness of breath with orthopnoea (sometimes basal crackles on auscultation of the chest)
- Raised jugular venous pressure
- Tachycardia with a third or fourth heart sound (gallop rhythm)

Thiazides have a limited diuretic effect, particularly where there is significant renal impairment, and they are not generally used on their own for salt/water clearance in this context. If there is clinically obvious fluid retention, loop diuretics are the best first-line treatment. In renal impairment, higher doses of loop diuretic than normal may be required. Accordingly, loop diuretic dosage should be titrated upwards to produce the required effects on fluid retention. In advanced renal impairment, doses up to 250mg furosemide per day may be required.

The influence of suspected renovascular disease on BP management

One of the major drawbacks of using ACE-Is and ARBs in CKD is their tendency to cause abrupt impairment of renal function in the presence of renovascular disease (see Chapter 8 for a more detailed description of this condition). The likelihood of occult renovascular disease may be inferred by the presence of large vessel atheroma at other sites (such as aortic aneurysm, femoral bruits or clinical peripheral vascular disease). It is important to make this assessment before prescribing ACE-Is and ARBs. Where the risk of occult renovascular disease is thought to be high, a hypertensive regime avoiding first-line use of ACE-I and ARBs may be preferred, even in the presence of proteinuria.

The influence of age on BP management

The NICE 2011 guidelines on the management of hypertension in the general population (in other words, people without known CKD) recommend that individuals under the age of 55 should receive an ACE-I first line and individuals over 55 years should receive a calcium channel blocker. In patients with CKD *but without significant proteinuria* (ACR<30mg/mmol), the same advice applies.

In patients with significant proteinuria, ACE-Is or ARBs should generally be used first line (see above). However, in very elderly subjects (over 80 years of age) the decision is complicated. Whilst several studies have shown that drugs influencing the renin/angiotensin/aldosterone system may have measurable benefits in the very elderly in terms of CV risk reduction and progression of CKD, their impact on risk reduction is less than in younger people. Furthermore, the elderly have a high incidence of occult renovascular disease and are therefore at greater risk of side effects from ACE-Is and ARBs compared to younger subjects. Obtaining serial blood tests to monitor the renal response to these drugs is burdensome (due to immobility, the need for transport to the clinic, etc.) outside the context of a clinical trial. In addition, this age group often have isolated systolic hypertension, which typically responds well to calcium channel blockers and diuretics.

Significant proteinuria is defined as ACR>30mg/mmol or PCR>50mg/mmol.

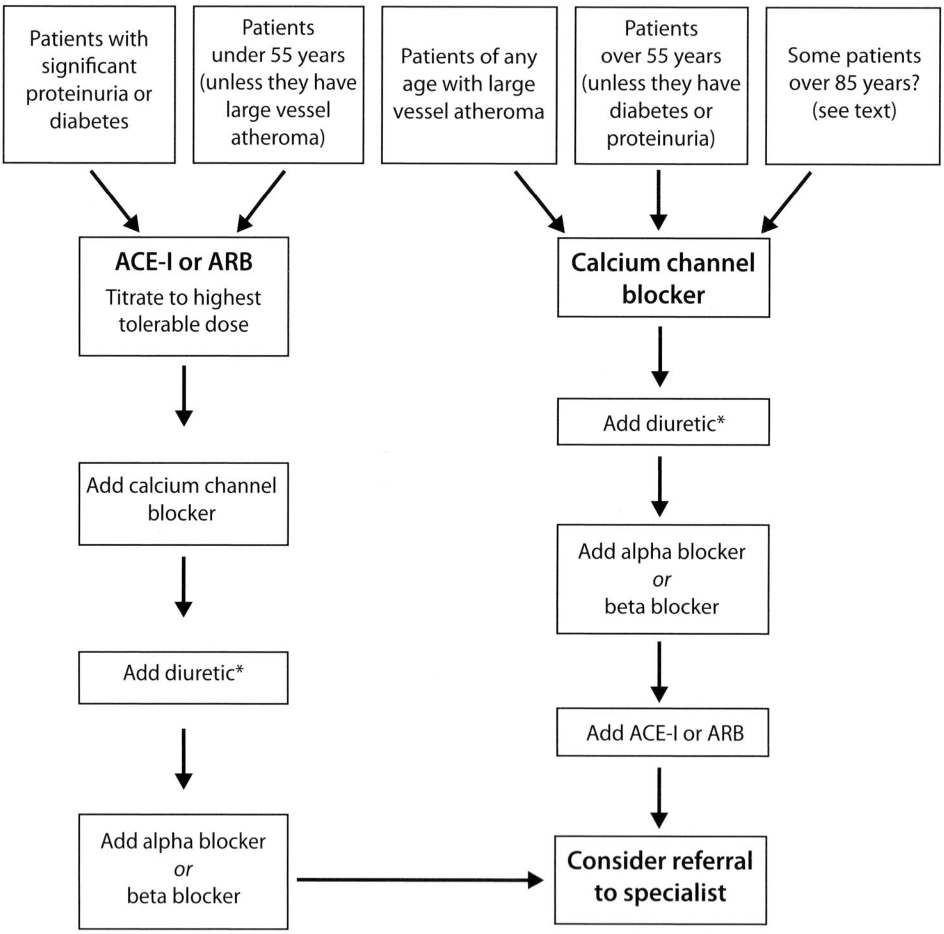

*Thiazide diuretic if eGFR>30ml/min.
Loop diuretic if eGFR<30ml/min or if signs of fluid retention are present.

Figure 9.1 *Management of hypertension in CKD: a guide for selecting the most appropriate agent according to the clinical circumstances. (Adapted from NICE hypertension guidelines 2011 and NICE CKD guidelines 2008)*

One therefore cannot be dogmatic about the choice of agents in the elderly hypertensive with CKD and proteinuria. It is increasingly recognised in treatment guidelines that standard advice may not be applicable in patients with a high burden of co-morbidities or in the very elderly. Expert advice (which is all the guidelines rely on, in the absence of robust scientific evidence) is to make a judgement on a case-by-case basis. Whilst this is a reasonable approach, it is difficult to square with the requirements of the QOF, which clearly encourages the use of ACE-Is and ARBs in all patients with proteinuria, regardless of age. This can be circumvented with the use of appropriate exemptions, but it illustrates the danger of using the QOF directly as a guide to best practice.

An algorithm to guide decisions on blood pressure management in CKD is given in Figure 9.1

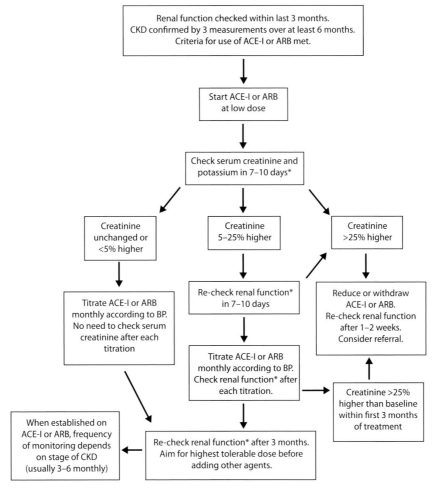

*If serum potassium >5.5mmol/l, reduce dose or withdraw ACE-I or ARB.

Figure 9.2 *Algorithm to explain how to use ACE-Is and ARBs safely in CKD.*

ACE-Is and ARBs in CKD

There has been a long-standing myth (which seems to be covalently bound in the minds of some practitioners) that ACE-Is should be avoided in CKD because they are 'nephrotoxic'. It is true that they can very occasionally cause acute interstitial nephritis in susceptible individuals (many drugs can), and they should be avoided during episodes of acute renal insult. But they are not nephrotoxic drugs in the way that NSAIDs clearly are.

The confusion has arisen because ACE-Is and ARBs can cause acute deterioration in renal function in people with renovascular disease. As hypertension and CKD may be the only clinical manifestations of this condition, drug formularies such as the BNF advise that drugs affecting the renin/angiotensin system need to be used with caution when treating hypertension in CKD. In practice, this means that renal function should be tested 7–10 days after starting an ACE-I or ARB in CKD. The algorithm in Figure 9.2 shows how the results should guide future management, and the diagram in Figure 9.3 shows the basis for this clinical advice. Note that a slight rise in serum creatinine is expected at initiation of these drugs because they cause a reduction in GFR, even in people without renal impairment. This is because they specifically reduce intraglomerular blood pressure and thus filtration pressure. Only when the reduction in renal function is marked should one conclude that there is an important haemodynamic effect due to occult renovascular disease.

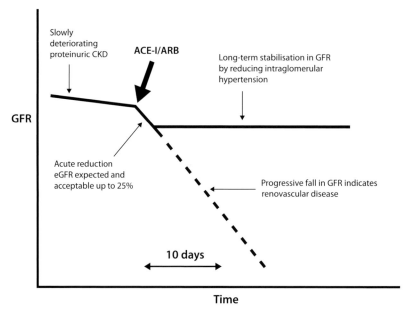

Figure 9.3 *The rationale for using ACE-Is and ARBs in slowly progressive, proteinuric CKD. An initial reduction in GFR is expected on starting these agents, but then the gradient of renal decline decreases over the medium to long term. Continued decline in renal function after starting these agents indicates renovascular disease. This is why renal function should be checked 7–10 days after starting treatment with an ACE-I or ARB.*

When to refer CKD patients for specialist advice on blood pressure

Once the diagnosis of CKD has been established (often with input from secondary care) it should become clear if optimal future management consists of no more than meticulous blood pressure control in an attempt to slow progression. Such management is best undertaken in primary care: an arrangement that is easier for the patient and more cost-effective. However, there are two circumstances when seeking further help from specialist services may be appropriate:

1. Where good concordance with treatment is likely, but patients fail to reach target blood pressure despite using three classes of anti-hypertensive agent.

2. When ACE-Is or ARBs cause acute deterioration of renal function, and renovascular disease is therefore suspected.

If a patient is intolerant of numerous classes of anti-hypertensives, it may be necessary to accept partial blood pressure control. This is reasonable clinical management and does not imply 'failure'. Nephrologists have at their disposal the same drugs as GPs and are no more likely to be able to make them acceptable to a patient.

Blood pressure targets in CKD

Targets for blood pressure control have changed frequently over recent years as evidence from large studies has become available. The old days of '100 plus the age' are long gone, and current recommendations are generally based on the J-shaped curve of outcome versus blood pressure, which is a consistent finding in these studies (an example is shown in Figure 9.4)

The evidence base for target recommendations in CKD is limited because the presence of CKD has been an exclusion criterion in many of the major studies upon which blood pressure recommendations in the general population have been based. However, because of the known impact of hypertension on CKD progression and the increased cardiovascular risk associated with CKD, the presence of CKD should warrant lower thresholds for starting treatment, a lower target blood pressure and more meticulous monitoring. NICE guidance on hypertension (2011) recommends that individuals with stage 1 hypertension (clinic BP 140/90 or higher, and daytime average BP 135/85 or higher) and renal disease should receive treatment to lower blood pressure (note conflict with NICE guidance on CKD, where this level of blood pressure is given as the target for treatment).

The risk of progression of CKD associated with high blood pressure is increased in people:

- Developing hypertension under the age of 55
- With diabetes of either type
- With heavy proteinuria (ACR>70, PCR>100)

Current blood pressure targets reflect the adverse impact of proteinuria and diabetes by setting more stringent targets in people with these factors (see Table 9.1).

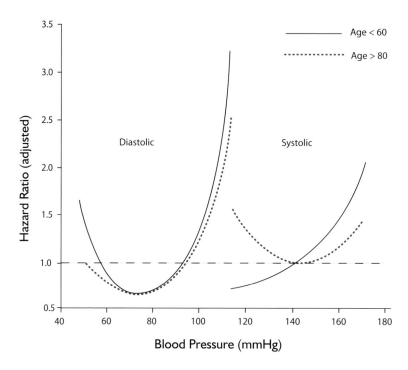

Figure 9.4 *The relationship between systolic and diastolic blood pressure and the risk of death and cardiovascular events. The graph shows the typical J-shaped curve, which has been shown by many studies. This example describes the effect of different levels of diastolic and systolic blood pressure on hazard ratio for death or cardiovascular events as found in the INVEST study. When the curves are below the line representing a hazard ratio of 1, the level of blood pressure is associated with reduced risk. When the curves are above this line, the risk is increased; a hazard ratio of 2 is equivalent to double the risk. In this graph, the curves for two age groups (patients under 60 and those over 80) are compared. Note that the risk of high systolic blood pressure is associated with greater risk in the younger age group. (Adapted from Denardo et al., 2010)*

Whilst these targets seem unequivocal and straightforward, it is worth reflecting on the QOF threshold for adequate blood pressure control in CKD – the implication being that a blood pressure in excess of the threshold counts as inadequate management. It is currently set at 140/85; so, as things stand, it is possible to meet NICE recommendations but fall short of achieving sufficient control to warrant remuneration.

It will be noted that current recommendations do not take account of age. This is contentious because there is little evidence that patients with CKD over 80 years of age benefit from having their blood pressure treated to a target of 140/90. A recent consensus document from the American Heart Association warned that the appropriate blood pressure target in the very elderly, and the agents used to attain it, should be guided by co-morbidities and patient tolerance. A blood pressure below 130/60 was likely to be harmful. Such recommendations rely on expert opinion rather than hard evidence from controlled trials.

Table 9.1 *Current blood pressure targets for people with CKD. Note that the targets are more stringent in the presence of diabetes or heavy proteinuria because of the known increase in vascular risk associated with these conditions. (Based on NICE 2008)*

Patient with eGFR less than 60ml/min plus:	Target blood pressure
No diabetes or proteinuria	120–140/90
Diabetes or ACR>70 (PCR>100)	120–130/80

Are there any other interventions that slow CKD progression?

As should now be clear, blood pressure control and judicious use of ACE-Is and ARBs (when proteinuria is present) are the big hitters in slowing progression of CKD. However, there are some other factors that may be important and should therefore be mentioned for the sake of completeness:

1. There is evidence that asymptomatic hyperuricaemia is associated with more rapid progression of CKD. Although it has not yet entered NICE guidelines, many would advocate the use of allopurinol in patients with CKD and confirmed hyperuricaemia. This is likely to be included in future guidelines.

2. There is good evidence that correction of acidosis in advanced CKD slows progression towards end-stage. This is probably only relevant in those patients who are already under regular review in a specialist centre in the pre-dialysis stage.

3. Improved glycaemic control is important in limiting progression of diabetic nephropathy.

4. For the record, it is worth noting that dietary protein restriction is no longer advocated as a way of slowing CKD (see Chapter 12).

Key points

- The key intervention that slows progression of CKD is meticulous blood pressure control to defined targets.
- Risk of progression is greater in people with diabetes or with proteinuria. Blood pressure targets are therefore more stringent in these people.
- ACE-inhibitors and ARBs retard progression of CKD in hypertensive people with proteinuria more than can be accounted for by blood pressure lowering alone.

References and further reading

Denardo, S.J., Yan Gong, Nichols, W.W. *et al.* (2010). Blood pressure and outcomes in very old hypertensive coronary artery disease patients: An INVEST Substudy. *American Journal of Medicine.* **123** (8), 719–26.

Goicoechea, M., Garcia de Vinuesa, S., Verdalles, U. *et al.* (2010). Effect of allopurinol in chronic kidney disease progression and cardiovascular risk. *Clinical Journal of the American Society of Nephrology.* **5** (8), 1388–93.

Kidney Disease Improving Global Outcomes (KDIGO). (2012). Clinical Practice Guidelines. www.kdigo.org/clinical_practice_guidelines

National Institute for Health and Clinical Excellence (NICE). (2008). Chronic Kidney Disease: National clinical guideline for early identification and management in adults in primary and secondary care. http://guidance.nice.org.uk/CG73

National Institute for Health and Clinical Excellence (NICE). (2011). Hypertension. http://guidance.nice.org.uk/CG127

The Renal Association. (2011). Detection, Monitoring and Care of Patients with CKD. www.renal.org/Clinical/GuidelinesSection/Detection-Monitoring-and-Care-of-Patients-with-CKD.aspx

Yaqoob, M.M. (2010). Acidosis and progression of chronic kidney disease. *Current Opinion in Nephrology and Hypertension.* **19** (5), 489–92.

10

When renal function takes a dip

As described in the preceding chapter, CKD is a progressive disease that can be successfully managed and monitored in a primary care environment. This chapter describes how we should proceed when the renal function of a patient under regular review shows an abrupt and unforeseen deviation from its former trajectory.

Although an abrupt change in eGFR may occasionally indicate some important change in the patient's health, it is generally the case that simply repeating the test shows spontaneous improvement to the previous baseline. The recognition that fluctuations of eGFR are quite usual in CKD (and that there is great variation in the degree of fluctuation from one individual to another) is a fairly recent development. It was once thought that CKD declined smoothly and predictably. Clinicians used to plot graphs of the reciprocal of creatinine (y-axis) against time (x-axis) for each patient, and would expect a straight line declining towards the x-axis, upon which they would base a prognosis and an expected time to dialysis. It is now accepted that eGFR is much less predictable. Transient changes in blood creatinine (and thus eGFR) are presumably due to minor changes in hydration status or dietary intake (serum creatinine can rise by more than 20% after a meal with a high meat content) although this has not been confirmed.

To ensure that these minor fluctuations in eGFR do not prompt an over-reaction, a significant change in renal function has been defined in the 2012 KDIGO guidelines as a change in CKD stage accompanied by a 25% or greater drop in eGFR. Even with this degree of change, a single uncharacteristic blood test should not prompt immediate referral for nephrological advice. The remedial action required may be quite simple, and some attempt should be made to identify a possible cause.

It is important to make the point at the outset that some unusual causes of CKD (such as glomerulonephritis) are characterised by episodes of relapse, which may manifest as an abrupt reduction in renal function. Whilst these conditions are usually under regular review in a nephrology clinic, occasional patients are missed, leading to potentially avoidable morbidity. Accordingly, when a surprise blood result is sustained on a repeat test, you should reacquaint yourself with the diagnosis of CKD, in particular re-checking the urine analysis (see Chapter 8 for further information on establishing a cause for CKD). If there are features to suggest active primary disease, prompt referral should be made. The remainder of this chapter will assume that the change in renal function is due to the effects of extraneous factors superimposed on otherwise stable underlying CKD.

'Acute on chronic' renal failure

A rapid decline of renal function in a patient with known CKD is often called 'acute on chronic' renal failure. Nowadays any insult to the kidneys is termed Acute Kidney Injury (AKI) by international convention. The causes of AKI are conveniently classified as follows:

Pre-renal insult: Dehydration (e.g. diarrhoea, vomiting, diuretics)
Systemic infection/toxaemia
Decrease in cardiac output (heart failure)

Direct renal insult: Nephrotoxic drugs
Radiocontrast
Renal embolisation/infarction

Post-renal insult: Bladder outflow obstruction

Pre-renal insult

Dehydration

In CKD, the normal homeostatic mechanisms controlling hydration status are impaired. Damaged kidneys have reduced capacity to concentrate the urine to preserve fluid during times of dehydration. Added to this, many of the drugs that are used in the management of CKD, notably diuretics and angiotensin converting enzyme inhibitors (ACE-Is), can interfere with adaptive mechanisms and increase susceptibility to acute renal damage. People with CKD are therefore at greater risk of AKI than people with normal kidneys.

A potential cause of dehydration is usually obvious – for example, pyrexial illness, diarrhoea, vomiting or a recent increase in diuretics. The physical signs of hypovolaemia are sometimes difficult to judge, because many of them are subjective. Nonetheless, one should look for the following:

Postural hypotension: This is one of the few objective signs available and is the most reliable indication of low circulating volume. It should be looked for in all cases of suspected hypovolaemia. It is assessed by measuring the blood pressure lying down and then, in the same arm, after two minutes standing. A fall in systolic blood pressure greater than 10mm/Hg is significant. In patients who cannot stand, lying and sitting blood pressure may have to suffice.

Dry mucous membranes: Especially in the elderly, the thirst sensation may be blunted, and dehydration can occur simply from failing to maintain sufficient fluid intake to compensate for the cause of dehydration. A dry tongue suggests this is the case. This is not a particularly reliable sign, since you may encounter individuals who snore or mouth-breathe and therefore have local desiccation of the mucous membranes without systemic dehydration.

Loss of skin turgor: Again, there is a certain amount of judgement required here, since the elderly have loose skin, which can mislead. It is best tested by squeezing the skin of the forehead between thumb and index finger to furrow the brow, rather than lifting skin on the back of the hand where the effect of age on skin laxity is more marked. If the skin does not quickly spring back on release, the patient may be dehydrated. A further useful sign, which hints at dehydration in a hospital setting, is the absence of oedema in patients who are known to have a low serum albumin (<30g/l).

Change in weight: Patients rarely know their weight with sufficient accuracy for this to be reliable for diagnosis in primary care. In a hospital setting, however, the best way to assess changes in hydration is by weighing the patient daily. Accordingly, patients with known CKD should always be weighed daily during an admission, when this is technically feasible.

A disproportionate rise in blood urea, compared to creatinine, is typical of dehydration and this can be useful to add weight to the clinical diagnosis. In severe cases, you may observe the effects of haemoconcentration on the pathology results. The usual signs of this are an increase in serum albumin and blood haemoglobin compared with previous recent results (where these are available).

It is usual for patients with known CKD to be receiving regular medication. Where dehydration is considered a risk, the drug regime should be reviewed and the following drugs should be suspended until the threat of dehydration has lifted:

- ACE-Is and angiotensin receptor blockers (ARBs)
- Loop and thiazide diuretics
- Non-steroidal anti-inflammatory drugs (NSAIDs)

Where the cause of the dehydration is likely to be self-limiting (such as transient diarrhoea), it may be reasonable to simply advise the patient to increase intake of fluid, particularly soups or broths (which contain salt and therefore restore circulating blood volume more efficiently than water alone).

The more advanced the CKD, the more susceptible the patient is to kidney damage as a result of hypovolaemia. Accordingly, if the dehydration is sufficient to give the clinical signs described above, or if there is a risk that the cause of dehydration will persist for more than a day or two, there should be a very low threshold for seeking specialist advice. In-patient rehydration may be required to prevent sustained AKI from developing.

Other causes of pre-renal insult

Systemic infection: People with CKD often show a transient decline in renal function during an intercurrent infection. This is partly because of loss of fluid as sweat, but it is also due to the effects of inflammatory mediators on renal perfusion and function. As is the case in dehydration, it is wise to suspend those drugs that affect renal compensatory mechanisms (see above). There should also be an attempt to identify the source of infection. Bacteriological analysis of the urine is advised, as urinary tract infection may not be clinically overt, especially in the elderly. Referral for advice is necessary if the change in renal function is marked, as in-patient rehydration and treatment of sepsis may be required.

Congestive cardiac failure: The combination of CKD and congestive cardiac failure (CCF) carries a poor prognosis and is very difficult to treat. Not only is renal perfusion reduced, threatening the adequacy of GFR, but the drugs used to treat CCF often have adverse renal effects. This is particularly true of diuretics, where a balance must be struck between pulmonary oedema on the one hand and diuretic-induced salt/water depletion on the other. There is no alternative but to monitor symptoms and renal function regularly, reducing the dose of diuretics if renal function deteriorates and increasing the dose if the patient reports worsening dyspnoea. The management of CCF in the context of CKD is covered in depth in Chapter 13.

Direct renal insult

Drugs

When the renal function of a patient with CKD declines unexpectedly, a review of the patient's recent medical history and drug prescriptions is mandatory. Common culprits for disturbing renal function are:

NSAIDs: These may be bought over the counter by the patient of their own volition, without the knowledge of their doctor. By blocking the action of prostaglandins in the kidneys, NSAIDs change the haemodynamics of flow through the glomerulus and cause a reduction in GFR. Where CKD is present, this may be sufficient to cause reduction in excretion of potassium (exacerbating hyperkalaemia), other markers of renal function (causing an acute rise in creatinine) and salt/water (causing hypertension and fluid overload).

Trimethoprim: This interferes with creatinine secretion by the renal tubule, leading to a spurious rise in serum creatinine levels. The effects can be readily reversed by stopping the drug.

ACE-Is and ARBs: A slight change in GFR is to be expected on starting these drugs because they reduce glomerular filtration pressure. However, patients with renovascular disease (which may not be clinically overt) may show an abrupt reduction in renal function. In CKD, renal function should be checked within two weeks of starting these agents to look for worsening renal function or hyperkalaemia. This is described in detail in Chapter 9.

Radiocontrast

It should be obvious if a patient has recently had an investigation requiring radiocontrast. Although use of ionic contrast agents has declined because of a high incidence of nephrotoxicity, even the newer non-ionic preparations (which are commonly used for angiograms and CT scans) still carry this risk. In patients with CKD, particularly those with diabetes, renal impairment caused by radiocontrast may be severe enough to cause dialysis-dependent renal impairment. The risk is greater, the more advanced the CKD; and the risk is further increased if the patient is hypotensive or dehydrated at the time of the radiological test.

The risk to renal function of using radiocontrast has to be weighed against the benefit to the patient of gaining the information provided by the radiological examination. Other investigations (notably magnetic resonance imaging or ultrasound) may be safer alternatives. Where it is decided that the use of radiocontrast is to the patient's overall benefit, certain measures can be taken to reduce the risk of adverse renal effects:

- Adequate hydration should be ensured prior to the investigation. The patient should be encouraged to drink at least 3 litres of fluid on the day leading up to the test. If this is not feasible, a litre of intravenous saline should be administered in the two hours prior to the examination.

- The radiologist should be advised of the presence of CKD so that they can minimise contrast dose.

- Iso-osmolar non-ionic contrast media of low viscosity, which are less nephrotoxic, should be used.

- Some people advocate prior administration of N-acetyl cysteine (orally, 600mg twice a day), starting a day before the procedure, or intravenously on the day of the procedure. However, trial evidence suggests that the benefit of this intervention is questionable.

- Adequate post-investigation monitoring of renal function is mandatory. Blood should be tested within a week of the procedure to check for effects on CKD, most notably potassium. Monitoring thereafter depends on the degree of renal impairment observed.

Damage due to arterial embolism

Displacement of an atheromatous plaque or thrombus may cause renal infarction, especially in patients with CKD due to renovascular disease where the ectatic, diseased renal artery is a common source of emboli. Embolisation typically causes a downward step in renal function to a new stable baseline (rather than a steady decline of function). It may be followed by subsequent emboli and thereby lead to a typically stepwise loss of renal function.

The diagnosis of arterial renal embolisation is usually inferred by the pattern of change in renal function in a patient with known atheroma. An ultrasound examination or a DMSA renogram may show evidence of cortical scarring, or patchy, asymmetric loss of renal mass. There is no useful specific intervention other than tightening-up control of vascular risk factors. Use of antiplatelet agents is rational, though evidence of benefit is sparse.

Referral to specialist services should be made if there is any concern about the degree of residual function. Where loss of renal function has been great, an urgent referral should be made, since very occasionally patients may benefit from a revascularisation procedure – but only if this is done within a day or two of the ischaemic insult.

Post-renal insult

Bladder outflow obstruction is common and may cause an abrupt deterioration in otherwise stable CKD. In men, the usual cause is prostatic enlargement and a history of recent worsening prostatic symptoms should always be sought. An enlarged bladder may be present on examination, often causing no concern whatever to the patient. Should the patient be at risk of obstruction but have no clinical evidence to suggest it, an urgent renal ultrasound will settle the issue; the finding of upper renal tract dilatation is usually unequivocal.

In the case of chronic bladder outflow obstruction, catheterisation is usually required and should be performed under in-patient supervision. This is because decompression after long-standing obstruction often leads to a brisk diuresis. In the presence of CKD, this needs careful monitoring to avoid hypovolaemia.

Referral to the urology department is generally required for all cases of urinary obstruction. This should generally be done urgently, since unrelieved obstruction can permanently damage the kidneys. In cases of CKD, this represents avoidable loss of valuable residual function.

Summary

When a patient's routine blood results for renal function deviate significantly from their usual course, Figure 10.1 below is a useful *aide mémoire*.

Even after considering the possible causes of abrupt functional loss using this algorithm, an answer may not be apparent. If this is the case, and the reduction in renal function continues to cause concern, referral for specialist advice is required – the urgency of the referral depends on the extent of renal deterioration.

Unfortunately, referrals to nephrologists are often sent in haste, before any of the issues addressed in this chapter have been considered (no more thought beyond 'Loss of renal function, query cause. Please do the needful'). In contrast, an adequate referral letter should include a summary of all the information used to answer the basic questions in Figure 10.1. With this to refer to, the nephrologist will arrive at a diagnosis much more quickly, which is in everyone's interest.

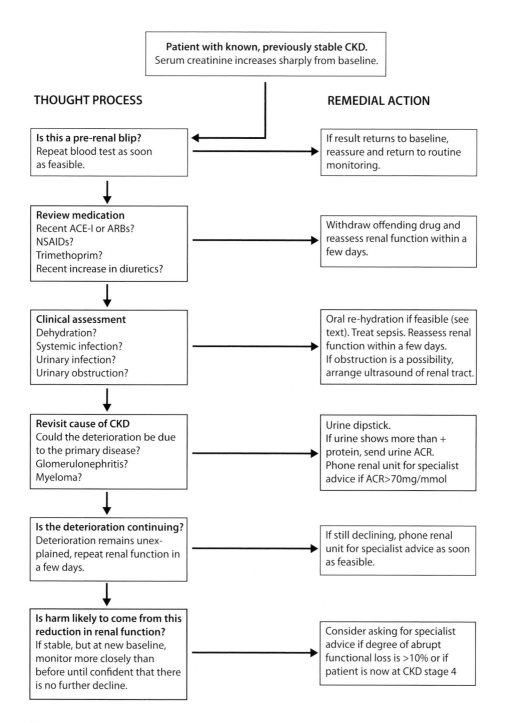

Figure 10.1 *Thought processes and remedial action when trying to identify the cause of an abrupt deterioration of renal function in a formerly stable CKD patient who is being monitored in primary care.*

Key points

- In CKD, a short-lived minor deterioration in renal function is common. A repeat test may be all that is required to provide reassurance.

- In patients with CKD, pre-renal elements (such as diet and hydration status) are the commonest causes for an observed deterioration in blood results.

- Drugs should be reviewed in all patients with CKD who have an intercurrent acute illness. Antihypertensive and diuretic drugs may need to be suspended.

- Referral for specialist advice may be appropriate when repeated tests of renal function show continued decline.

Further reading and references

Kidney Disease Improving Global Outcomes (KDIGO). (2012). Clinical Practice Guidelines. www.kdigo.org/clinical_practice_guidelines

Lamiere, N.H. & Vanholder, R.C. (2005). 'Acute renal failure: pathophysiology and prevention' in *Oxford Textbook of Clinical Nephrology.* 3rd edition. (eds A.M. Davison, J. Stewart Cameron, J.P. Grunfeld *et al*.). 1445–64. Oxford: Oxford University Press.

National Institute for Health and Clinical Excellence (NICE). (2008). Chronic Kidney Disease: National clinical guideline for early identification and management in adults in primary and secondary care. http://guidance.nice.org.uk/CG73

Long-term systemic effects of CKD: Blood and bones

As we saw in Chapter 6, CKD in its early stages has important systemic effects, notably on cardiovascular risk. Other systemic effects may occur as a direct consequence of impaired renal function and the build-up of toxic waste in the bloodstream, but these occur much later in the natural history of CKD (stage 4–5) when most CKD patients are under specialist review. A comprehensive account of the systemic effects of advanced CKD is therefore of limited relevance to the non-specialist. However there are two exceptions: renal anaemia and renal bone disease. In a patient with CKD and anaemia, how do we tell if the latter is due to their CKD or to some other unrelated cause? When patients with CKD have low-impact fractures, how do we know if they have renal bone disease or osteoporosis (which is common in the same population which is susceptible to CKD)? And if osteoporosis is suspected, how do we manage it in the context of CKD?

Renal anaemia

The anaemia of CKD is primarily due to failure of production of renal-derived erythropoietin. This usually occurs at stage 4–5 CKD, but in patients with diabetes it may occur earlier – for reasons that remain unclear.

Anaemia is common in the elderly. CKD is also common in the elderly, but because its severity may be difficult to judge (see Chapter 7), a causal link with anaemia may not immediately be identified. Furthermore, patients in this age bracket often have co-morbidities (such as cardiac failure or ischaemic heart disease), which are worsened by inadequate correction of anaemia. Identifying and treating renal anaemia in the elderly is therefore important. Even the very elderly, including those with severe co-morbidities who are unsuitable for renal replacement therapy, benefit from management of their anaemia in the context of a conservative care programme.

Where there is a possibility that a patient may benefit from anaemia management, referral to the renal unit is recommended. However, for the renal unit to decide if treatment of renal anaemia is appropriate, the practitioner making the referral needs to undertake some initial assessment and management.

Firstly, it is not safe to assume the connection between CKD and anaemia without pausing to consider other common causes of anaemia. Typically, the anaemia of CKD is normochromic and normocytic, but may be microcytic. The rate of decline in haemoglobin is very slow – over months or even years. Platelet and leucocyte populations are unaffected. If the anaemia has features that differ from this, it may have another cause. A history of overt blood loss or other relevant symptoms (such as malaena, indigestion or bowel disturbance) should also be sought.

Haematinics should be checked. The following tests are required:

- Serum ferritin (should be >200mcg/l)
- Percentage transferrin saturation (should be >20%)
- C-reactive protein (should be within normal range)
- Vitamin B12 (should be within normal range)
- Red cell folate level (should be within normal range)

Care should be taken when interpreting the ferritin level, as this is an acute phase protein and it rises in conditions of systemic inflammation. Measuring the C-reactive protein at the same time is a good way to judge any effect of inflammation.

Patients with CKD are often deficient in iron (possibly due to a combination of low-grade occult blood loss and poor dietary intake) and oral iron (ferrous sulphate 200mg t.d.s. or equivalent) should therefore be commenced when the anaemia is first identified. This is true even when the ferritin level is apparently within the 'normal' range; it has been shown empirically that patients with renal anaemia need a serum ferritin level above 200mcg/l to optimise haemopoesis. Absorption is better when oral iron is taken on an empty stomach and is reduced by phosphate binders, antacids and drugs suppressing gastric acid secretion.

If, despite two months of oral iron, the patient remains anaemic (haemoglobin below 10mg/dl or symptomatic), referral to the renal unit should be considered. All renal units have departments dealing with renal anaemia, usually run by a team of nurse specialists. They are responsible for coordinating the administration of intravenous iron and erythropoietin stimulating agents (ESAs), the latter commonly referred to as EPO. Often, these departments distribute the prescriptions, arrange refrigerated delivery and advise patients of changes in dosage.

The first task undertaken by the specialist team is to correct any iron deficiency. This may persist even after prolonged oral iron supplementation because iron absorption from the gastrointestinal tract is often poor. Iron is therefore given by intravenous infusions, until the serum ferritin exceeds 200mcg/l. If the patient remains anaemic despite having an adequate ferritin level the next step is to start ESA therapy.

A specialist service is mandatory when establishing patients on ESAs. All available ESAs are administered by injection, and patients or carers can usually be trained by specialist nurses to undertake these injections themselves. Usual dosing regimes involve injections monthly, fortnightly, weekly or twice-weekly, depending on the preparation being used and the haemopoetic response.

The patient's haemoglobin should start to respond within a month, usually with an associated improvement in well-being. Common causes of a poor response include underlying systemic malignancy or inflammation, continued haematinic deficiency, primary bone marrow disease, hyperparathyroidism and unrecognised blood loss.

The target haemoglobin level for CKD patients on ESAs is currently 10–12g/dl. Correcting haemoglobin to the level of healthy individuals has been empirically found to worsen outcomes in dialysis patients; the target applied to all CKD patients is therefore just short of normal. Once established on an ESA, regular monitoring and titration of dosage requires continued specialist input. Although the anaemia specialist nurses maintain surveillance, primary care practitioners have an important role to play in administering the ESA injections to those unable to treat themselves, monitoring blood pressure, and performing monitoring blood tests (thus enabling patients to avoid making repeated trips to hospital).

The anaemia team monitors iron stores (assessed by serum ferritin and transferrin saturation) and administers top-up IV iron courses as required. The blood pressure is monitored closely, as this may rise when starting ESAs, necessitating an increase in anti-hypertensive medication. Usually, conventional anti-hypertensive treatment can restore blood pressure control, but occasionally the dose of ESA (and hence the degree of anaemia correction) is limited by its hypertensive effect.

Coordinated management of anaemia has been one of the greatest advances in CKD management in the last 30 years. Some of us remember the sallow, ghostly faces of dialysis patients from the pre-ESA era who maintained haemoglobins around 6g/dl and who assumed profound fatigue, poor cardiovascular reserve and absent libido to be part of the renal failure syndrome. Anaemia management has since been shown to improve CKD patients' perception of their quality of life, and there is much evidence to show its beneficial effect on cardiovascular function and longevity. ESAs remain expensive, but the emergence of generic preparations onto the market is likely to drive costs down in future.

CKD-mineral-bone disorder (CKD-MBD)

To the non-specialist, the importance of CKD-MBD (the term that has replaced renal osteodystrophy) is its tendency to increase the risk of fractures and cause cardiovascular calcification, both of which may increase mortality in patients with advanced CKD.

Biochemical evidence of hyperparathyroidism is often evident by stage 3 CKD. However, routine monitoring of parathyroid hormone (PTH) in primary care, which has been recommended in the past, is not necessary at this stage. Routine biochemical monitoring of the renal function of CKD 3a–3b patients is sufficient to reveal significant imbalances of calcium/phosphate, which may need correction. At stage 4 CKD it may be appropriate to measure PTH every six months. But in patients who have chosen not to be candidates for renal replacement therapy (due to age or co-morbidity), the value of routine screening for bone disease, in the absence of bone symptoms, is questionable.

The clinical burden of CKD-MBD

Bone disease

Abnormal quality and quantity of bone can lead to an increased risk of fractures in patients with CKD. Hip fractures are seen approximately twice as often as in patients without CKD. The risk of fracture is increased in patients who have had longer exposure to dialysis. Mortality of patients with CKD-MBD who have a hip fracture is about double that of patients without CKD.

The pattern of bone disease in CKD has changed over the last 20 years. In the past, high bone turnover was predominant. Such hyperparathyroid bone disease led to bone deformities in children, short stature and reduced quality of life. Nowadays, the gross skeletal abnormalities (renal rickets) described in the past are exceptionally rare. Instead, there is also a high prevalence (40–70% of individuals with CKD stage 4–5) of low-turnover bone disease, which weakens the bone and increases fracture risk. Such adynamic bone diseases may be the result of an aging population and a side effect of recognition and treatment of rapid bone turnover. Effective treatment of CKD-MBD therefore requires attention to both high- and low-turnover bone diseases and aims to steer a course between the two.

Vascular calcification

Extraosseous calcification is very common in patients with advanced CKD. Its prevalence increases with severity of renal dysfunction and the length of time a patient remains on renal replacement therapy. Although calcium may deposit in any soft tissue, cardiovascular calcification has been the focus of most attention.

The arterial calcification associated with CKD-MBD is rather different from that seen in the general population. In the latter, calcification is greatest in the arterial intima, where it forms a part of atherosclerotic plaques. These predispose to ischaemic events such as myocardial infarction. In CKD-MBD, there is a greater proportion of calcification in the arterial media, which causes vascular stiffness and hypertension.

Because available techniques cannot reliably distinguish between the two patterns of calcification, there is an ongoing debate about the relevance of each to adverse outcomes in CKD patients. Nevertheless, based on studies of the outcomes associated with vascular calcification (whatever its distribution), there is little doubt that there is a strong association with cardiovascular events and mortality.

Management of CKD-MBD

The key to management of CKD-MBD is to prevent excessive PTH production early in the disease. Early intervention is preferred because a chronically stimulated parathyroid gland can become autonomous, and late attempts to control its activity are much less effective. Parathyroid stimulation can be minimised by keeping the calcium level in the normal range, managing hyperphosphataemia and replacing vitamin D (which is deficient due to reduced synthesis by the kidneys). Dietary phosphate restriction (see Chapter 12) and the use of phosphate binders are the main means of phosphate control.

Phosphate binders are compounds that have a high affinity for dietary phosphate but are not absorbed. The phosphate is therefore bound in the gut and excreted in the faeces. Accordingly, all phosphate binders must be taken with meals to ensure optimal mixing with food. There are a number of options. It is usual to use calcium containing phosphate binders first line, as these are inexpensive and have the theoretical advantage of supplementing calcium, thus reducing parathyroid stimulation. However, they may also contribute to vascular calcification. Accordingly, non-calcium-containing binders are available (sevelamer and lanthanum). These avoid the risk of vascular calcification, but at considerable financial cost. Aluminium hydroxide is a cheap, effective non-calcium containing alternative, but it presents the theoretical risk of aluminium toxicity.

A key intervention to prevent CKD-MBD is to prevent excessive PTH production. The level of PTH should not be suppressed to normal levels because this may increase the risk of adynamic bone disease. Instead, treatment aims to keep the PTH level below nine times the normal level. This can be achieved using two approaches:

1. Oral vitamin D supplements (such as alfacalcidol): These suppress PTH production and are prescribed for patients with stage 3–4 CKD. Their use is limited by their tendency to cause hypercalcaemia. This occurs because vitamin D increases calcium absorption via the gut, particularly when patients are also taking calcium-containing phosphate binders. Calcium/phosphate monitoring is required at least every two months, with careful titration of the dose of vitamin D supplement and calcium containing phosphate binders. This is best done in a specialist setting.

2. Cinacalcet: This directly suppresses PTH production by mimicking the effect of calcium on receptors within the parathyroid gland (hence it is termed a 'calcimimetic'). By acting in this way, it has the advantage over vitamin D analogues of not causing troublesome hypercalcaemia. It is effective in reducing PTH level and can reduce the need for surgical parathyroidectomy. Although it has been supported by the National Institute for Health and Clinical Excellence (NICE), it is expensive compared to vitamin D and calcium, and this has tended to restrict its use.

Osteoporosis

Both osteoporosis and CKD are common in older people. CKD itself is likely to predispose to the development of osteoporosis, as patients often have poor nutritional intake and are relatively immobile. However, very few studies have addressed osteoporosis in CKD because of the greater clinical concern surrounding CKD-MBD. Bone mineral density criteria cannot be used to diagnose osteoporosis in this population since all forms of renal bone disease produce low 'T scores'. Bone biopsy might be used (and has its advocates) but most UK nephrologists consider this much too invasive and not a useful guide to subsequent therapy. It is generally assumed that the effect of CKD-MBD is quantitatively much more significant in CKD than osteoporosis, and therapy to prevent fracture risk in CKD should therefore be primarily directed at CKD-MBD.

This raises the question of whether or not it is advisable to treat, or give prophylaxis against, osteoporosis in patients with known CKD. There is no simple answer to this question. A balance needs to be struck between the perceived risk of osteoporosis and the risks of using the available treatments for osteoporosis in the presence of CKD. It is usually advised (for example, by the British National Formulary) that bisphosphonates should be avoided in patients with an eGFR of less than 30ml/min. This advice is based on a few isolated cases of acute renal impairment in patients receiving bisphosphonates, but there have been no rigorous trials looking at the risk of these drugs in CKD. Furthermore, there is no trial evidence to suggest that bisphosphonates offer any benefit in patients with CKD. Nonetheless, where prophylaxis against osteopaenia is particularly important (for instance, in long-term steroid therapy), most clinicians would support the use of bisphosphonates in CKD, provided the dose is cut to half when the eGFR is below 15ml/min.

Gonadal hormones and their analogues probably help preserve bone even in CKD, but evidence in patients is limited. Raloxifene, which acts upon the oestrogen receptors and should theoretically benefit women regardless of renal function, can improve spine bone density in dialysis patients. This treatment might therefore be used in women without an elevated risk of clotting. In hypogonadal men, testosterone could be considered.

Denosumab (human monoclonal antibody to Rank-Ligand) has recently been licensed for treatment of osteoporosis. It is a potential treatment for patients with CKD, as it is not cleared by the kidney but is instead metabolised by the reticuloendothelial system. In addition, denosumab has been shown to be safe for three years in patients with eGFR down to 15ml/min. Prospective studies will define the potential renal safety for this agent in patients with even more severe renal failure. However, it is unlikely that a study showing its effectiveness in patients with CKD will be undertaken because of the absence of outcome measures that are not also influenced by CKD-MBD.

Key points

- Anaemia is common in CKD stage 4, and assessment of haemoglobin forms an important part of routine monitoring in CKD.
- Iron deficiency is common in CKD. Oral iron should be tried, but intravenous iron infusions are often required because of poor absorption of iron from the gut.
- ESAs improve quality of life in people with renal anaemia, even when they are very elderly or are considered unsuitable for renal replacement (dialytic) therapy.

- Referral for specialist management of renal anaemia should be considered when the patient is symptomatic or has a haemoglobin below 10g/dl despite oral iron supplementation.

- Patients with unexplained anaemia and apparently mild CKD should be discussed with the renal unit – they may benefit from anaemia management.

- CKD-mineral-bone disorder (CKD-MBD) may predispose to vascular calcification and increase cardiovascular morbidity.

- Management of CKD-MBD should be initiated before it becomes overt, and should be routine at stage 4 CKD.

- Management of osteoporosis in CKD is difficult and of doubtful benefit.

- Prophylaxis against osteoporosis in very high-risk patients is reasonable. Bisphosphonates are probably safe up to an eGFR of 15ml/min.

References and further reading

Gordon, P.L. & Frassetto, L.A. (2010). Management of Osteoporosis in CKD Stages 3 to 5. *American Journal of Kidney Diseases.* **55** (5), 941–56.

Kidney Disease Improving Global Outcomes (KDIGO). (2009). Guideline for Chronic Kidney Disease Mineral Bone Disorder. *Kidney International.* **76** (suppl 113) S1-S130.

National Institute for Health and Clinical Excellence (NICE) (February 2011). Anaemia management in people with chronic kidney disease. Guideline CG114.

12

Diet and nutrition in CKD

The importance of diet and nutrition in renal disease is long established. In the past, CKD patients extended their pre-dialysis lives by rigorous dietary restriction, most notably of protein, on the basis that lower protein intake led to less urea production and therefore less 'uraemia'. It was also thought that protein restriction slowed disease progression in CKD. In patients with advanced CKD, dietary restriction was particularly severe, and they regarded it as a major reduction in their quality of life. Anyone who has tried protein-free bread can readily understand their feelings.

Following several large studies, protein restriction has been discredited as a therapeutic intervention. In fact, it has emerged that malnutrition is the predominant problem in CKD, becoming more prevalent as the disease progresses. Accordingly, dietary advice in CKD now focuses more on safeguarding adequate nutrition, even from an early stage, and patients are no longer subjected to rigorous inappropriate dietary restrictions. Dietary advice for most people with CKD follows the same principles as for the general population; they are encouraged to eat a wide variety of foods and only alter their normal diet when specific problems are identified.

Diagnosing undernutrition

Undernutrition occurs in 28–48% of the pre-dialysis CKD population and is associated with increased morbidity and mortality. Its prevalence increases with decreasing GFR and increasing age. Vigilance in identifying evidence of undernutrition is therefore especially important in elderly patients.

It is easy to miss undernutrition in the context of CKD if you rely solely on blood results. Patients with poor protein calorie intake generate little urea and, as their muscles waste, they make less creatinine. An undernourished patient may therefore have advanced CKD, disguised by unimpressive measurements of blood urea, serum creatinine and eGFR. Direct clinical assessment is required if undernourishment is not to be missed.

A diagnosis of undernutrition should be considered in patients presenting with unintentional weight loss of >10% in the last six months and in patients with BMI<18.5kg/m² (Renal Association guidance, 2007). A low serum albumin, although non-specific, is another useful indicator of inadequate protein-calorie intake.

If undernutrition is suspected, steps should be taken to boost protein-calorie intake along the usual lines (using dietary supplements). In more advanced disease (CKD stage 4 or more), it becomes more complicated to take remedial action because of other dietary issues (phosphate, potassium, etc.) and patients should be referred to a registered dietician for nutritional assessment and support. All renal units have a specialist dietician.

Dietary restriction in CKD

Patients with CKD should not be advised to follow a low protein diet, but to aim for a normal protein intake of approximately 0.8–1g/kg ideal body weight per day. Some patients with excessive protein intake may need to reduce their protein intake to this level.

Although dietary restriction should be minimised, there are two specific dietary constituents that patients with advanced CKD may need to restrict: phosphate and potassium. In both instances, dietary restriction should only be instigated when blood tests show high levels (i.e. potassium greater than 5.0mmol/l and phosphate greater than 1.8mmol/l).

Phosphate

Hyperphosphataemia is associated with increased cardiovascular morbidity and mortality in CKD. It is unusual for hyperphosphataemia to become a problem before CKD stage 4, when it is an important driver of CKD mineral bone disorder (see Chapter 11).

Phosphate is particularly rich in high-protein foods, notably the following:

- Hard cheeses, eggs
- Processed meats such as pâté and luncheon meat
- Offal
- Nuts
- Some oily fish such as mackerel, sardines, pilchards (tuna and salmon are acceptable)

It is important to ensure that those patients who need to reduce their phosphate intake do not reduce their protein intake excessively. It is therefore recommended that patients with hyperphosphataemia due to CKD are reviewed by a specialist dietician in the context of pre-dialysis (low clearance) care, as described in Chapter 17. Dietary restriction alone is usually insufficient to overcome hyperphosphataemia and phosphate binders are required to chelate dietary phosphate in the gut, as described in Chapter 11.

Potassium

Dangerous hyperkalaemia is a feature of late CKD and is one of the indications for dialysis. However, patients in the pre-dialysis stages of CKD may develop hyperkalaemia, which can be managed without resorting to dialysis. Whilst dietary potassium intake is a major determinant of serum potassium levels, non-dietary causes of hyperkalaemia are much more common and should be excluded in the first instance. The common causes are:

- Angiotensin converting enzyme inhibitors, angiotensin receptor blockers, spironolactone
- Non-steroidal anti-inflammatory drugs
- Metabolic acidosis caused by advanced CKD (check serum bicarbonate)

Where a low-potassium diet is required to maintain a serum potassium level below 6mmol/l, review by a specialist renal dietician is recommended. It is difficult for patients to avoid potassium completely, and advice is needed on which potassium-containing foods are occasionally allowable and which should be avoided altogether. Foods containing high levels of potassium include:

- Most fruits (notably bananas, which should be avoided altogether)
- Fruit juices
- Many vegetables (notably potatoes, which should be boiled with a change of water halfway through cooking to remove potassium)
- Coffee
- Breakfast cereals containing bran, nuts and dried fruit
- Snack foods (potato crisps, nuts, chocolate)

Other dietary issues in CKD

Hypertension

There is no evidence that managing hypertension by dietary modification changes the outcome of CKD. Nonetheless, because of the importance of hypertension in the prognosis of CKD, it is rational to advise on dietary modification along the usual lines:

- Maintain ideal weight for adults (BMI: 20–25kg/m^2)
- Reduce salt intake to <100mmol sodium/day (<6g salt or 2.4g sodium/day)
- Limit alcohol consumption to ≤3 units/d for men and ≤2units/d for women
- Consume at least five portions of fruit and vegetables daily (within the limits set by the need for potassium restriction)
- Reduce intake of total and saturated fat

According to the National Diet and Nutrition Survey undertaken by the Department of Health in 2011, current average salt intake in the UK is approximately 8g/day, much of which comes from processed foods. Although achieving lower salt intake presents a challenge, there is no doubt that average salt intake in the UK has steadily fallen over the last decade. Switching from an unrestricted diet to one containing less than

100mmol sodium (equivalent to about 6g of salt) per day has been shown to reduce systolic pressure by about 7mmHg and diastolic pressure by about 4mmHg. It is reasonable to suppose that this effect extrapolates to CKD patients, although the necessary studies have not been undertaken. One barrier to achieving a reduced sodium intake in CKD patients is that the salt substitutes often used in sodium reduction programmes are not suitable, due to their high potassium content. A useful tip is to flavour food with black pepper, herbs and spices, which can cover the blandness of salt-reduced food.

Obesity

Obesity (BMI>30kg/m^2) is associated with increased cardiovascular risk and thus contributes to the overall risk to a patient with CKD. Management of obesity has been shown to reduce the rate of decline in GFR in early CKD. Morbid obesity (WHO class 3, BMI>40kg/m^2) is itself a cause of proteinuria and progressive renal impairment. Weight reduction in these individuals reduces proteinuria and slows renal decline. Management of obesity in CKD is much the same as in individuals with normal kidney function.

Diabetes

In patients with either type 1 or type 2 diabetes, good glycaemic control (in which attention to diet plays an important part) delays the onset of nephropathy. However, once nephropathy is established, there are no specific dietary measures that influence disease progression. Patients with diabetes have a particular challenge when combining their diabetic dietary advice with restrictions imposed by their CKD. Accordingly, specialist dietary advice is required at CKD stage 4.

Key points

- Dietary modification in stage 1–3 CKD is largely aimed at cardiovascular risk reduction.
- Tight protein restriction is no longer recommended as a means of slowing progression of CKD.
- Undernutrition is common in stage 4–5 CKD, and assessment of nutritional status is an important aspect of management.
- Specialist dietary advice forms an important element of pre-dialysis (low clearance) care at stage 4 CKD.

References and further reading

British Renal Society. Eating Well For Your Kidneys. Educational resource produced by the British Renal Society. www.britishrenal.org/getattachment/CKD-Forum/Educational-Resources/CKD--Nutrition-Leaflet.pdf.aspx

Curhan, G.C. & Mitch, W.E. (2008). 'Diet and kidney disease' in Brenner and Rector's *The Kidney*. 8th edition. (eds B.M. Brenner & S.A. Levine). 1817–47. Philadelphia, USA: Saunders Elsevier.

Sadler, K., Nicholson, S., Steer, T. *et al.* (2012). National Diet and Nutrition Survey – Assessment of dietary sodium in adults (aged 19 to 64 years) in England, 2011. Department of Health. http://transparency.dh.gov.uk/2012/06/21/sodium-levels-among-adults

13

Managing heart disease in the context of CKD

It is very common for CKD and heart disease to occur in the same individual. The presence of CKD complicates the management of common heart conditions, but clinical guidelines usually ignore this association. Accordingly, this chapter explains the interplay between cardiac disease and CKD, and how this combination of co-morbidities should best be managed.

Congestive cardiac failure

The incidence of both congestive cardiac failure (CCF) and CKD increases with age. Furthermore, treatment of CCF with diuretics and drugs acting upon the renin/angiotensin/aldosterone system (RAAS) may, in some individuals, contribute to worsening renal function. A number of aetiological factors are common to CCF and CKD, such as diabetes and hypertension. CKD is also a marker for generalised atheroma and is therefore likely to coexist with ischaemic heart disease. In more advanced CKD, renal anaemia may contribute to cardiac decompensation. It is therefore no surprise that the combination of CCF and CKD is common in clinical practice. This presents a challenging clinical problem, which deserves special consideration.

Several studies have shown that the presence of CKD in patients with decompensated CCF is an independent marker for poor prognosis. Approximately 45% of patients hospitalised with CCF develop deterioration in renal function, and those with CKD are at greater risk of this deterioration. Studies have shown that even small renal function changes in patients with CCF are associated with adverse outcomes. One study showed that, in patients admitted with decompensated CCF, the relative risk of death was nearly three times more in patients with an eGFR<44ml/min when compared to those with an eGFR>76ml/min. In fact, the existence of CKD is a stronger predictor of mortality than is ejection fraction as assessed by echocardiogram.

So close is the link between worsening renal function and adverse cardiac outcomes that the term 'cardiorenal syndrome' has been coined to describe the situation in which decompensated cardiac function leads to an abrupt deterioration in renal function.

The interplay between heart and kidneys

Traditionally, the close relationship between worsening renal function and decompensated CCF has been attributed to haemodynamic changes, particularly those that affect renal perfusion. This is based on the understanding that renal perfusion is determined by cardiac output and vascular resistance. In CCF, cardiac output is reduced. This reduces renal perfusion and stimulates intrarenal responses, notably the RAAS, which lead to salt and water retention. Although this mechanism is intended to restore renal perfusion, the failing heart is unable to adjust to the increased volume load. This leads to a self-perpetuating cycle of worsening cardiac decompensation, worsening renal perfusion and thus worsening excretory function.

Whilst this explanation seems reasonable, the mechanism is actually more complex. We know this because studies have shown little correlation between low ejection fraction and worsening renal function. Accordingly, other factors have been implicated, including:

- **Diuretic use**: In CCF, intravascular hypovolaemia may exist even in the face of increased total body fluid. Fluid in the extravascular space (clinical oedema) may lead clinicians to prescribe more aggressive diuretic regimes, which can worsen intravascular depletion and thus further reduce renal perfusion.
- **Venous congestion**: Renal perfusion is influenced by the pressure gradient across the kidney. Patients with CCF, who have raised right atrial pressure and often a relatively low arterial pressure therefore have a reduced pressure gradient. Renal perfusion is thus compromised, leading to renal dysfunction.
- **Renovascular disease**: Atheromatous renovascular disease is present in about 30% of elderly patients presenting with CCF. This is only haemodynamically significant in a small proportion of these patients, but contributes to the risk of an adverse response to drugs acting on the RAAS.
- **Chronic inflammation**: Both CKD and CCF are associated with upregulation of cytokines such as tumour necrosis factor and interleukin-6. High levels of these molecules in patients with CCF and CKD are predictive of adverse outcomes. It has been hypothesised that increased venous pressure caused by CCF leads to gut wall oedema and translocation of bacterial endotoxin. This has direct effects on vascular resistance and thus renal perfusion.

Managing CCF in the context of CKD

The management of CCF against the background of CKD is very challenging. Treating the symptoms of salt and water overload, which are prominent in advanced CCF, often leads to intravascular volume depletion, hypotension and worsening renal function. Withdrawing treatment may improve renal function and restore blood pressure, but at the cost of worsening oedema and respiratory compromise. So what is the clinician to do?

The first task is to review the medication. It is important that the patient is not exposed to NSAIDs, which worsen renal impairment and contribute to salt and water retention. If blood pressure is low (systolic<120mmHg), anti-hypertensive drugs that have no value in CCF (such as calcium channel blockers or alpha blockers) should be stopped in favour of agents that have a dual effect in both CCF and hypertension.

Diuretics

Oral diuretics are important in managing CCF. However, they often have unreliable absorption when CCF is severe because of the presence of gut oedema. Higher oral doses may be prescribed to achieve a diuresis, although there is evidence that high doses of oral diuretics are associated with worse outcomes. Accordingly, in-patient administration of intravenous diuretics may be required when fluid retention is severe. A slow intravenous infusion of diuretic is preferred to repeated boluses because this allows time for extravascular fluid to equilibrate and is less likely to cause intravascular volume depletion. Once the response to intravenous diuretics has been optimised, subsequent conversion to an appropriate oral regime can maintain this equilibrium.

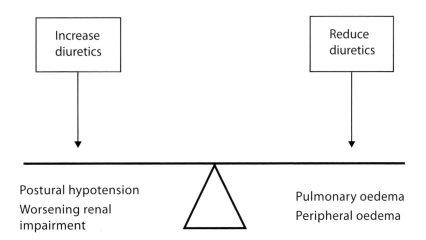

Figure 13.1 *Management of CCF in CKD: the therapeutic window when using diuretics becomes narrower as CKD and CCF advance. Careful titration of diuretic dosage is required to strike a balance between intravascular volume depletion and overload.*

Patients with CKD are often resistant to loop diuretics. Where high doses (>160mg furosemide per day) are insufficient to produce an adequate diuresis, a better response can be attained by adding a thiazide diuretic such as metolazone. This inhibits sodium absorption throughout the nephron, thus augmenting the effects of loop diuretics. The resulting diuresis can be rapid and profound, so this approach is best carried out under direct supervision of secondary care (usually as an in-patient). The patient should be weighed daily, aiming for a loss of no more than 0.75kg per day. Faster loss of fluid risks hypovolaemia and worsened renal impairment.

Whilst diuretics are the mainstay of treatment of CCF in CKD, their value is limited by symptomatic hypotension (particularly in the older patient) and worsening renal function (see Figure 13.1). Patients therefore need very careful monitoring of blood pressure (with particular vigilance for a postural drop in pressure) and blood chemistry, coupled with regular titration of diuretic dose. The frequency of monitoring will depend on individual circumstances. Community outreach specialist cardiac services, if available, are particularly valuable in carrying out this surveillance.

ACE-Is and ARBs

The addition of drugs acting on the RAAS should only be initiated when the patient is volume replete. This should be assessed clinically. Even in patients with an appropriate fluid balance, initiating angiotensin converting enzyme inhibitors (ACE-Is) and angiotensin receptor blockers (ARBs) may cause an initial reduction in renal function. However, there is clear evidence that these drugs improve survival in patients with CCF. Provided the serum creatinine does not rise more than 25% in the first 14 days after starting treatment, this diminution of renal function should be tolerated. Where renal decline is greater than this, it may be safer to minimise the dose or even withdraw the ACE-Is and ARBs.

The greatest benefit comes from the highest tolerable dose of ACE-Is or ARBs. The dose should therefore be titrated upwards where possible. Tolerance of these drugs in CCF is limited by symptomatic hypotension or hyperkalaemia.

Other drug therapies

Beta blockers are of proven benefit in chronic CCF. In the context of severe CCF causing renal impairment and hypotension, their benefits are unknown. They should be tried, provided they do not contribute to hypotension. Spironolactone is also of proven benefit in advanced CCF. However, the value of beta blockers in CKD is limited by their tendency to cause hyperkalaemia, particularly when prescribed in conjunction with ACE-Is or ARBs.

Fluid removal by filtration and dialysis

In patients with CKD and severe, decompensated CCF refractory to the above measures, fluid can be removed from the blood without relying on renal excretory function. Haemofiltration is one such approach. With this technique, a central venous catheter is inserted (usually into the right atrium via the internal jugular vein), and blood is pumped via an extracorporeal circuit through a filtration membrane. By presenting the blood to the membrane surface under pressure, intravascular fluid is 'squeezed out' and discarded. Haemofiltration can be undertaken as a slow, continuous process to minimise the risk of hypovolaemia and to allow time for fluid from the tissues to equilibrate with circulating blood. Similar slow fluid removal has been undertaken in CCF by using peritoneal dialysis (see Chapter 17). However, haemofiltration and peritoneal dialysis have not been subject to adequate trials to evaluate their effects on ultimate outcome.

These approaches are clearly highly specialised and are available only in an intensive care unit or a renal unit. Deciding to embark on such measures in advanced CCF with CKD can be difficult. Hospital-based continuous therapies are usually only offered if there is a good chance that fluid removal will lead to sustained improvement in cardiac function. Nonetheless, long-term dialysis treatment (usually peritoneal dialysis, which is less stressful for the cardiovascular system) can be deployed to treat advanced chronic heart failure that has proved refractory to drug treatment alone. This should be seen very much as a last resort, requiring thorough appraisal of the patient's overall quality of life and assessment of the likelihood that dialysis will improve this.

Acute coronary events in CKD

As described in Chapter 6, there is a high incidence of coronary heart disease in patients with CKD and they are therefore at high risk of acute cardiac events. The presence of CKD can complicate the diagnosis and management of these.

Measurement of serum troponins is now established as an important aspect in management of patients presenting with acute coronary syndromes. An elevated level of serum troponins indicates acute myocyte necrosis, and the degree of elevation helps to identify patients who are at increased risk of death or recurrent myocardial infarction. The test has therapeutic value in that it identifies those patients for whom aggressive drug and interventional therapy improves outcome.

However, the appropriate use of these enzymes in patients with CKD is less clear. Elevated serum troponins are observed in patients with renal insufficiency who do not have clinical evidence of myocardial damage or symptoms. About 20% of dialysis patients have an elevated troponin T, but only 0.4% have an elevated troponin I. The mechanism for this sustained elevation is unclear. It may be due to left ventricular hypertrophy, endothelial dysfunction, loss of myocyte membrane integrity, cardiac stretching or impaired renal excretion. In asymptomatic patients with advanced CKD, an elevated troponin should therefore be interpreted with caution.

When patients with CKD present with acute coronary syndromes, there is a risk that an elevated troponin level may be misinterpreted as indicating the presence of myocardial infarction. This risk can be reduced to a minimum by using troponin I, rather than troponin T, and by using a higher cut-off level for a positive test. Because of the variation in normal range of troponin I between laboratories, it is not useful to give a reference range applicable in CKD here. In addition, serial measurements should be undertaken in order to observe a change in level over 6–18 hours. In CKD, such a sequential change is a better indicator of an acute event than a single, slightly elevated result. The prognostic significance of a definite rise in troponin level is much the same as in patients without CKD, and should be treated as such. Management of a confirmed acute coronary syndrome or myocardial infarction in CKD does not differ significantly from that in patients with normal renal function

Concern is often expressed about undertaking angiography and primary coronary intervention in patients with CKD because of the risk of contrast nephropathy (see Chapter 10). Pre-intervention hydration and cessation of undesirable drugs (such as those affecting the RAAS) may not be possible in the acute event. However, the risk of delaying or avoiding coronary intervention is much greater than the risk of an acute kidney injury, the latter usually being reversible. Accordingly, CKD should not be used as a reason *not* to intervene. In dialysis patients, of course, loss of residual renal function is less of a problem, and radiocontrast therefore does little significant harm.

Key points

- The combination of CKD and CCF is common in clinical practice because they share aetiologies and compound each other.
- The presence of CKD worsens outcomes in CCF.
- In patients with decompensated CCF and CKD, admission for slow infusion of intravenous diuretic is often required to achieve equilibrium.
- ACE-Is or ARBs should be continued in all but the most extreme cases.
- Short-term treatment with haemofiltration may be indicated where the cause of cardiac decompensation is potentially reversible.
- CCF in CKD can sometimes be managed by dialysis after careful assessment.
- Elevation of troponin levels should be interpreted with caution in CKD; serial measurements are required.
- The risk of contrast nephropathy in CKD is no reason to deny patients the benefits of coronary intervention.

References and further reading

Cowie, M.R., Komajda, M., Murray-Thomas, T. *et al.* (2004). Prevalence and impact of worsening renal function in patients hospitalised with decompensated heart failure: results of prospective outcomes study in heart failure (POSH). *European Heart Journal.* **27** (10), 1216–22.

De Silva, R., Nikitin, N.P., Witte, K. *et al.* (2005). Incidence of renal dysfunction over 6 months in patients with chronic heart failure due to left ventricular systolic dysfunction: contributing factors and relationship to prognosis. *European Heart Journal.* **27** (5), 569–81.

Han, J.H. (May 2005). Interpretation of cardiac troponin levels in patients with chronic kidney disease and suspected acute coronary syndromes in the emergency setting. *Emergency Medicine Cardiac Research and Education Group (EMCREG).* 3.

Hillege, H.L., Nitsch, D., Pfeffer, M.A. *et al.* (2006). Renal function as a predictor of outcome in a broad spectrum of patients with heart failure. *Circulation.* **113** (5), 671–78.

Shiplak, M.G. & Massie, B.M. (2004). The clinical challenge of cardiorenal syndrome. *Circulation.* **110** (12), 1514–17.

14

Diabetes and renal disease

Of the causes of CKD, diabetes and in particular diabetic nephropathy, deserve a chapter to themselves. Diabetic nephropathy is the most common cause of renal disease in the United Kingdom, accounting for approximately 20% of cases of end-stage renal failure. As the incidence of diabetes increases and its management is increasingly devolved away from specialist centres, medical and nursing staff in primary care settings are increasingly responsible for detecting and managing the renal issues associated with it. Since most of the interventions that affect prognosis are only effective at the earliest stages of the disease, it is important for non-specialists to be fully aware of the pitfalls of diagnosis and management.

Natural history of diabetic nephropathy

Diabetic nephropathy is the renal manifestation of the systemic microangiopathy that characterises diabetes of either type. Table 14.1 shows how the clinical features change as the disease progresses.

The earliest effect of diabetic renal disease is hyperfiltration, where the GFR may rise significantly (although this change is not evident clinically). Continuing damage to the glomerular basement membrane leads to leakage of small amounts of albumin (the smallest circulating protein molecule) into the urine. This low level of proteinuria is only quantifiable using the urine albumin:creatinine ratio (ACR). Conventional urine testing sticks and protein:creatinine ratio (PCR) are not sufficiently sensitive (see Chapter 5). Microalbuminuria is defined by an ACR greater than 2.5mg/mmol in males and 3.5mg/mmol in females but less than 30mg/mmol in either sex. In type 1 diabetes, approximately 20–30% of individuals develop microalbuminuria after having diabetes for an average of 15 years.

In about 50% of people with microalbuminuria, the disease progresses and proteinuria increases to the level where conventional dipsticks can detect it (equivalent to ACR>30mg/mmol or PCR>50mg/mmol). This is when true diabetic nephropathy is said to have commenced. The proteinuria may reach nephrotic levels (PCR>500mg/mmol with oedema and hypoalbuminaemia) in about 3% of diabetics. The onset of clinical proteinuria is associated with a decline in GFR and a tendency towards hypertension. Thereafter, renal function declines towards end-stage disease at a very variable rate; some patients remain off renal replacement therapy for 20 years, whilst others decline rapidly and require dialysis or a transplant in one to two years.

Table 14.1 *The natural history of diabetic nephropathy.*

Stage of diabetic nephropathy	GFR	Albuminuria	Blood pressure
Renal hyperfiltration	Elevated (>100ml/min)	Absent	Normal
Microalbuminuria	Normal	ACR 2.5–30mg/mmol in males and 3.5–30mg/mmol in females	High normal
Macroalbuminuria (clinical nephropathy)	Often reduced	ACR>30mg/mmol PCR>50mg/mmol	High
Renal failure	Decreasing to end-stage renal disease	May be nephrotic (PCR>500mg/mmol)	High

Although it was once thought that diabetic nephropathy was less common in type 2 diabetes, current evidence suggests that the renal risk is equivalent in both types. The time to proteinuria from the onset of diabetes, and the time to end-stage renal disease from the onset of proteinuria, is similar in type 1 and type 2 disease.

Factors that increase the risk of an individual with diabetes developing nephropathy are: poor glycaemic control, hypertension and dyslipidaemia. It will be noted that these are the same factors that influence the development of generalised vascular disease. This is why management of diabetic nephropathy is largely aimed at reducing systemic vascular risk.

Establishing the diagnosis of diabetic nephropathy

In a diabetic patient presenting with CKD, diabetic nephropathy has the following characteristics:

- History of diabetes (type 1 or 2) for at least two years
- Proteinuria (a prerequisite of the diagnosis)
- Hypertension (usual)
- Microvascular complications at other sites (usual)

Where a patient with diabetes has renal impairment but no proteinuria, an alternative diagnosis should be sought. In type 1 diabetes, the onset of proteinuria within five years of the onset of diabetes is most unusual and should raise the possibility of a primary glomerular lesion (such as glomerulonephritis). Non-visible haematuria is not a feature of diabetic nephropathy. Where a urine reagent strip detects blood, an alternative diagnosis is likely.

In type 1 diabetes, it is unusual for nephropathy to develop before signs of microvascular complications elsewhere. If a type 1 diabetic develops renal impairment and proteinuria when retinopathy is absent, a specialist opinion should be sought in order to exclude an alternative diagnosis. In type 2 diabetes, the relationship is less well defined. One study showed that only 50% of type 2 diabetics with biopsy-proven diabetic nephropathy have retinopathy.

Other chronic renal diseases have an increased incidence in people with diabetes and may be misdiagnosed as diabetic nephropathy. These include:

- Hypertensive nephropathy
- Atherosclerotic renal artery stenosis
- Chronic pyelonephritis
- Glomerulonephritis

The features of these conditions, and how they may be differentiated from diabetic nephropathy, are outlined in Chapter 8.

What microalbuminuria tells you – and what you should do about it

Microalbuminuria strongly predicts the development of diabetic nephropathy. Patients with type 1 diabetes and microalbuminuria have a 21-fold increased risk of developing diabetic nephropathy (i.e. ACR>30mg/mmol with or without low eGFR) compared to those without microalbuminuria. For people with type 2 diabetes, the increased risk is 9-fold.

Around 40–50% of patients with type 2 diabetes who have developed microalbuminuria die of cardiovascular disease. This is three times the risk compared to patients with no microalbuminuria. It is now established that intensifying glycaemic and blood pressure control, and in particular using drugs that act on the renin angiotensin aldosterone system (RAAS), can reduce or abolish microalbuminuria – with a commensurate improvement in prognosis.

Accordingly, microalbuminuria should be regarded as a useful way of detecting those people with diabetes who are at high risk of renal and cardiovascular disease at a time when intervention can still make a difference. All patients with diabetes should be routinely screened for microalbuminuria at least once a year. Because false positive results may occur in the presence of poorl controlled hypertension or following exercise, a single abnormal result is insufficient to determine that microalbuminuria is present. Therefore, it is necessary to obtain three abnormal results over at least six months to be sure that microalbuminuria is present.

Once the presence of microalbuminuria has been established, the following measures need to be taken:

- **Meticulous glycaemic control**: There is good evidence to suggest that tight glycaemic control slows or prevents the progression of microalbuminuria to overt nephropathy. Accordingly most guidelines recommend maintenance of haemoglobin A1c (HbA1c) below 7% when microalbuminuria is detected.
- **Use of angiotensin converting enzyme-inhibitors (ACE-Is) or angiotensin receptor blockers (ARBs)**: Numerous studies have shown that, in both type 1 and type 2 diabetes, the use of drugs acting on the RAAS is of benefit in delaying progression from microalbuminuria to overt nephropathy. When microalbuminuria is detected, these drugs should be started (even in the absence of hypertension) and titrated up to the highest tolerated dose.
- **Meticulous blood pressure control**: Where hypertension is present (which is nearly always the case), this should be treated aggressively. The target blood pressure in diabetes is lower than in non-diabetic individuals, to reflect their increased cardiovascular risk (see Chapter 9). Should ACE-Is or ARBs not be tolerated for whatever reason, maintenance of blood pressure control with other agents is still beneficial (albeit less so) in reducing the onset of morbidities associated with microalbuminuria. It is worth noting that the particular beneficial effect of drugs acting on the RAAS on renal and cardiovascular prognosis in diabetes does not apply when patients have non-proteinuric CKD that is due to some other cause.

Delaying progression to renal failure

Once the ACR rises above 30mg/mmol (clinical diabetic nephropathy), there is usually an inexorable decline towards end-stage renal disease. However, the rate of progression can be influenced by the same measures that are deployed at the onset of microalbuminuria. The impact of blood pressure control is particularly important, whereas evidence that tight glycaemic control slows progression of overt nephropathy (once it has developed) is less compelling.

Agents acting upon the RAAS have clear beneficial effects on slowing progression of proteinuric diabetic renal disease (see Figure 14.1). The use of ACE-Is and ARBs above the maximum recommended anti-hypertensive doses has been shown to increase their antiproteinuric effects in patients with type 2 diabetes who have macroalbuminuria, without having any appreciable effect on blood pressure control. It is not known if this translates into better long-term cardiovascular or renal outcomes.

Since the combination of ACE-Is and ARBs inhibits the RAAS and reduces proteinuria more effectively than either agent alone, it would seem logical to use a combination of these drugs to further improve the patient's prognosis. Studies undertaken to date have not shown any advantage in a combination of ACE-I and ARB over monotherapy in reducing long-term vascular outcomes, and the combination has been associated with a higher incidence of adverse effects. Most nephrologists would restrict use of a combination of these drugs to situations when proteinuria is itself a problem (as in nephrotic syndrome).

Another potential approach is the use of direct renin inhibitors (such as Aliskiren). Studies indicate that these can reduce microalbuminuria effectively in diabetes. However, it is yet to be determined whether Aliskiren is a valuable alternative to currently available RAAS inhibitors in reducing progression of renal disease. A study of the effect of a combination of direct renin inhibitors with either ACE-Is or ARBs on mortality and cardiovascular events was undertaken recently (ALTITUDE study, Novartis Inc). This was terminated before completion because worse vascular and renal outcomes in both diabetic and non-diabetic patients were observed. The manufacturers of Aliskiren have issued notification that combining this drug with either ACE-Is or ARBs is contraindicated.

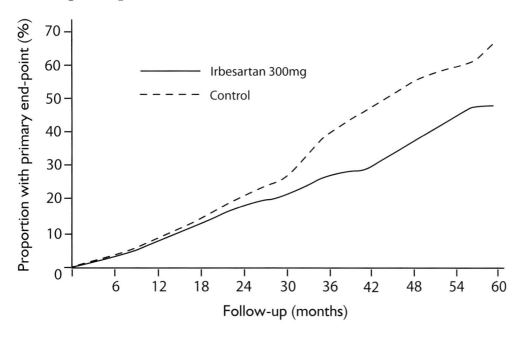

Figure 14.1 *ACE-Is and ARBs slow progression of diabetic nephropathy. This graph shows the proportion of people with type 2 diabetes who reached primary end-points (doubling of serum creatinine, end-stage renal disease or death) whilst being treated for hypertension to a target of 135/85. Comparison is made between a cohort whose antihypertensive regime included the ARB irbesartan and a control group taking other antihypertensive drugs needed to achieve the same target blood pressure plus a placebo. Note that after 18 months the curves diverge as the rate of decline towards the primary end-points is slowed in the irbesartan group. A similar 'renoprotective' effect in proteinuric diabetic kidney disease has been shown with other ARBs and with ACE-Is. The protection is not afforded by blood pressure lowering alone (as this is the same in both groups) and is a particular effect of drugs acting on the renin/angiotensin system. (Graph adapted from Lewis et al., 2001)*

Advanced CKD in diabetes

People with diabetes and advanced renal excretory dysfunction present particular management problems. Serial measurements of HbA1c, which are normally so valuable in glycaemic management in diabetes, may be unreliable in advanced CKD. This is because some of the methods used to measure HbA1c, are affected by elevated concentrations of urea, leading to false elevations in the HbA1c level. Other factors that affect the accuracy of these assays include reduced red blood cell lifespan, iron deficiency, accelerated erythropoiesis due to administration of erythropoietin, and metabolic acidosis. As a result, HbA1c levels tend to underestimate the quality of glycaemic control in diabetic patients.

Oral hypoglycaemic agents

Knowledge of the metabolism of oral hypoglycaemic agents in patients with CKD is essential, given that significant toxicity, including prolonged hypoglycaemia, can be associated with some of the drugs. The use of oral hypoglycaemic agents in CKD is summarised in Table 14.2.

Table 14.2 *Hypoglycaemic agents currently used in the treatment of diabetes. This table summarises their safety in mild, moderate or severe CKD.*

Drug	Mild (eGFR 30–60ml/min)	Moderate (eGFR 15–30ml/min)	Severe (eGFR<15ml/min)
Metformin	Yes	No	No
Sulphonylureas (gliclazide, glipizide)	Yes	Caution	No
Metaglinides	Yes	Yes	Caution
Pioglitazone	Yes	Yes	Yes
Acarbose	Yes	Yes	No
DPP-4 inhibitors: Sitagliptin Vildagliptin Saxagliptin Linagliptin	Yes Yes Yes Yes	No No Yes (reduced dose) Yes	No No Yes (reduced dose) Yes
GLP-1 analogues Liraglutide Exenatide (BD) Exenatide (weekly)	Yes Yes Yes	No Yes (dose adjustment) No	No No No
Insulin	Yes	Yes	Yes

Sulphonylureas

The basic principles of sulphonylurea metabolism can be summarised as follows:

- Chlorpropramide is eliminated almost exclusively by the kidney. It can accumulate in patients with impaired kidney function and contribute to the development of hypoglycaemia.
- Gliclazide has weak active metabolites that are excreted in the urine and accumulate in patients with impaired kidney function.
- Glimepiride is primarily metabolised by the liver, with renal excretion of active metabolites.
- Glipizide and tolbutamide are metabolised by the liver and primarily excreted in the urine as inactive metabolites. However, each has one metabolite that may have weak hypoglycaemic activity.

Due to the risk of hypoglycaemia, sulphonylureas should generally be avoided in advanced CKD. However, glipizide, gliclazide and tolbutamide may be used if necessary, provided careful monitoring of blood glucose can be assured.

Biguanides

Metformin is primarily excreted unchanged in the urine. A rare side effect of treatment with metformin is lactic acidosis. The risk of this is said to be greater in the presence of advanced CKD, and metformin should be withdrawn in these circumstances. The degree of CKD at which metformin should be stopped is poorly defined. A judgement therefore needs to be made – balancing the potential risks of continuing the drug against the well-known benefits of maintaining glycaemic control, particularly in obese individuals. Most guidelines recommend that an alternative agent should be used when the eGFR is less than 30ml/min, but others would draw the line at 20ml/min. There is no evidence base to provide a definitive answer.

Thiazolidinediones

These agents enhance tissue sensitivity to insulin and suppress hepatic glucose production. Rosiglitazone and pioglitazone are highly protein bound, primarily to albumin, and almost complete metabolised by the liver. Rosiglitazone has inactive metabolites and less than 1% of the original compound is excreted in the urine; pioglitazone is associated with three active metabolites. With both agents, the accumulation of the parent drug or the major metabolites does not occur in the setting of renal insufficiency.

Notwithstanding this, thiazolidinediones are associated with heart failure and the development of oedema. They should therefore be avoided in patients with advanced kidney failure, particularly if they have evidence of pre-existing heart failure.

Alpha-glucosidase inhibitors

Acarbose slows carbohydrate absorption from the gastrointestinal tract and reduces postprandial blood sugar peaks. Acarbose and its metabolites accumulate in renal insufficiency. Although an increased risk of hypoglycaemia has not been documented, acarbose should be avoided when the eGFR is less than 25ml/min.

Meglitinides

Nateglinide and repaglinide stimulate insulin secretion. Repaglinide is principally metabolised by the liver, with less than 10% being renally excreted. Hypoglycaemia may occur in patients with advanced CKD, and maintenance doses should be lower in these patients. Initiation of treatment should be with 500μg daily, and close monitoring of blood glucose levels is essential as the dose is titrated.

Nateglinide is hepatically metabolised, with renal excretion of active metabolites. This drug can be used in advanced CKD, but with enhanced attention to glycaemic control.

Glucagon-like peptide (GLP)-1 analogues/agonists

These agents bind to specific GLP-1 receptors, which stimulate increased insulin secretion by pancreatic islet cells. Exenatide and liraglutide are relatively new agents and experience of their use in CKD patients is limited. The dose of the twice-daily preparation of exenatide can be adjusted for use in moderate CKD, but otherwise this class of agent should be avoided when renal function is more than mildly impaired.

Dipeptidylpeptididase (DPP)-4 inhibitors

These agents inhibit DPP-4, which inactivates GLP-1. This has the effect of increasing insulin secretion and lowering glucagon secretion. They are usually used in combination with metformin or sulphonylureas which limits their value in advanced CKD. Whilst sitagliptin and vildagliptin should be avoided, saxagliptin and linagliptin are safe and have licences for use in advanced CKD. They may require dose adjustment, as outlined in their data sheets.

Insulin

Because oral hypoglycaemic agents are difficult to use in advanced CKD, early initiation of insulin treatment is frequently required. Advanced CKD is associated with resistance to insulin but also reduced insulin degradation and excretion. These two opposing effects often lead to erratic glycaemic control as CKD approaches end-stage disease. There is little that can be done about this effect other than to increase the frequency of monitoring and to favour insulin regimes that can easily be titrated according to blood sugar readings.

End-stage renal disease in diabetes

People with diabetes present their own special issues when they require renal replacement therapy. It is convenient to describe these issues here, but the following section may best be read in conjunction with Chapter 17 where the various modalities of treatment used for end-stage CKD are described in greater depth.

The major issue for patients with diabetes and end-stage CKD is that, at all ages, their mortality is higher than those with renal failure from other causes (see Figure 14.2), largely due to a greatly increased incidence of cardiovascular disease. Measures to reduce cardiovascular risk therefore remain central to management of these individuals, even when the kidneys have failed

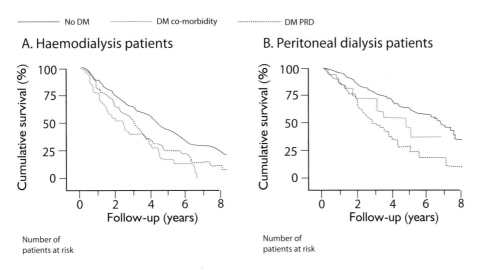

Figure 14.2 *Kaplan-Meier graphs of survival of patients on haemodialysis (A) and peritoneal dialysis (B). Comparison is made between patients with no diabetes mellitus (no-DM), diabetes as a co-morbidity but not the cause of CKD (DM co-morbidity), and those with diabetes as their primary renal disease (DM PRD). (Source: Schroijen et al., 2011)*

Transplantation

The best treatment for a patient with CKD due to diabetic nephropathy is a simultaneous pancreas–kidney (SPK) transplant. Patients receiving the combined transplant survive longer than those receiving a kidney alone. The acceptance criteria are more rigorous than for a kidney transplant alone and they are shown in Table 14.3

Table 14.3 *Criteria for consideration for simultaneous kidney pancreas transplantation. These are the current criteria in use in the author's unit, but minor local differences may apply elsewhere in the UK.*

Inclusion criteria	Exclusion criteria
Insulin-dependent diabetes	Inability to comply with follow-up
eGFR <20ml/min or on dialysis	Active malignancy (excludes skin)
Age <65 years	Body mass index >30kg/m²
Limited cardiovascular disease	Active HIV infection
Body mass index <30kg/m²	Ongoing drug or alcohol abuse
	Ongoing major psychiatric illness

Patients receiving an SPK transplant should expect their kidney to last just as long as a kidney alone transplant (see Chapter 17). About 90% of SPK transplant recipients are insulin-free one year after transplantation and about 85% remain so after three years. Patient and graft survival rates continue to improve with ongoing changes to surgical techniques and postoperative management. Currently, the majority of SPK-recipients should expect to derive a useful contribution to glycaemic control after five years.

The operation involves anastomosing the donor kidney to the recipient iliac vessels on one side and the pancreas with its attached segment of duodenum on the other (see Figure 14.3). The exocrine secretions of the pancreas have to be disposed of safely. This is achieved either by draining them into the recipient's bladder or (as shown in Figure 14.3) into the recipient's small bowel. The favoured technique varies between transplant units.

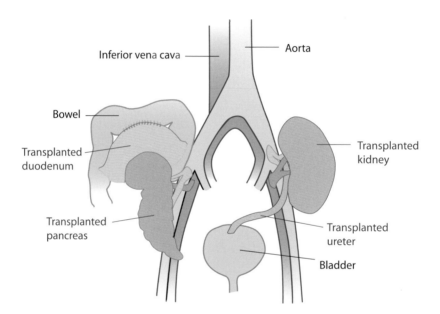

Figure 14.3 *Simultaneous kidney–pancreas transplantation. Note that the pancreas is transplanted in conjunction with the donor duodenum, which is then attached to the recipient's bowel to permit drainage of exocrine pancreatic secretions. Drainage used to be achieved via the bladder, but this technique caused chemical cystitis and has now been abandoned.*

Because of the high incidence of vascular disease in diabetes, many patients reaching end-stage CKD are considered 'high-risk' for transplantation. This may be because of coronary disease (thus limited post-transplant prognosis) or atheroma in the major pelvic vessels (which makes engraftment technically difficult and prone to vascular complications). Although outcomes for kidney transplantation in diabetics are worse than in non-diabetics, the possibility of a transplant should be explored and each individual should be carefully counselled about the chances of success. Twenty years ago it was a general rule that transplantation should not be offered to diabetics on the basis that outcomes were so poor. This is no longer the case.

Post-transplant management of people with diabetes differs little from the usual. The immunosuppressive regimes are similar – steroid minimisation is good practice in all transplanted patients. However, treatment with steroids may cause deterioration of glycaemic control, requiring closer monitoring.

Haemodialysis

Correction of uraemia on starting dialysis diminishes insulin resistance and enhances insulin degradation. Close monitoring of blood glucose is therefore required when dialysis is started. The net effect on glycaemic control will vary from patient to patient, thereby necessitating individualised therapy. In general, insulin-based regimes are preferred to those using oral hypoglycaemic agents because of the variable clearance of the latter by dialysis.

Haemodialysis requires reliable vascular access in the form of an arteriovenous fistula. This in turn requires the presence of good-quality arteries in the forearms. People with diabetes have a higher incidence of complications associated with their vascular access. One common problem is 'steal syndrome', which occurs when arterial blood is diverted away from the hand through the fistula. Because of diffuse peripheral arterial disease, the reduction in blood flow renders the fingers ischaemic, leading to pain and loss of function.

There was once a belief that haemodialysis should be avoided in people with diabetes because heparinisation during dialysis increased the risk of retinal haemorrhage. This is no longer the case: outcomes with peritoneal dialysis and haemodialysis in people with diabetes are similar.

Peritoneal dialysis

The dialysate used in peritoneal dialysis contains a high concentration of glucose in order to draw fluid from the circulation by osmosis. However, once the osmotic gradient across the peritoneal cavity has equilibrated, there follows reverse diffusion of glucose and water back into the circulation. This glucose load affects glycaemic control and requires careful adjustment of insulin regimes. It may lead to considerable weight gain, as the glucose is assimilated from the blood. Although insulin can effectively be administered intraperitoneally, this approach is rarely used in the UK.

Successful peritoneal dialysis requires dexterity to undertake the dialysate exchanges. This may be lacking in people with diabetes who have peripheral neuropathy or are visually impaired through retinopathy, and this limits its application to some individuals.

Key points

- Diabetes is a common cause of CKD and is increasing in incidence.
- The key to management is early identification of proteinuria through targeted screening in a primary care setting and meticulous blood pressure control with high-dose ACE-Is or ARBs.

- At end-stage renal disease, people with diabetes face particular management problems, and outcomes are generally less favourable than in non-diabetics.

- Outcomes are steadily improving and people with end-stage disease can expect a good quality of life, particularly if they are suitable to receive a simultaneous pancreas–kidney transplant, which is the treatment of choice.

References and further reading

Joy, M.S., Cefalu, W.T., Hogan, S.L. & Nachman, P.H. (2002). Long-term glycemic control measurements in diabetic patients receiving hemodialysis. *American Journal of Kidney Disease.* **39** (2), 297–307.

KDOQI. (2005). Clinical practice guidelines for cardiovascular disease in dialysis patients. *American Journal of Kidney Disease.* **4** (Suppl 3) S1.

Lewis, E.J., Hunsicker, L.G., Clarke, W.R. *et al.* (2001). Renoprotective effect of the angiotensin-receptor antagonist irbesartan in patients with nephropathy due to type 2 diabetes. *New England Journal of Medicine.* **345** (12), 851–60.

Lubowsky, N.D., Siegel, R. & Pittas, A.G. (2007). Management of glycemia in patients with diabetes mellitus and CKD. *American Journal of Kidney Disease.* **50** (5), 865–79.

National Institute for Health and Clinical Excellence (NICE). (2008). Type 2 diabetes. National Clinical Guideline for management in primary and secondary care (update). Guideline G62.

Schroijen, M.A., Dekkers, O.M., Grootendorst, D., Noordzij, M., Romijn, J.A., Krediet, R.T., Boeschoten, E.W., Dekker, F.W. & the NECOSAD Study Group (2011). Survival in dialysis patients is not different between patients with diabetes as primary renal disease and patients with diabetes as a co-morbid condition. *BMC Nephrology.* **12**, 69.

15

Fertility and pregnancy in the context of CKD

Women of fertile age may develop CKD. The most common causes in this age group are diabetic nephropathy, reflux nephropathy/chronic pyelonephritis, chronic glomerulonephritis and inherited renal disease. Should a patient with CKD wish to start a family, they may enquire about the likelihood of an uncomplicated pregnancy and the effects of a pregnancy on their renal prognosis. Accordingly, it is important for the non-nephrologist to have some basic understanding of how pre-existing CKD is likely to affect the outcome.

Fertility and contraception

Early CKD (stage 1–3) has little or no impact on fertility. Advanced renal disease (stage 4–5) is associated with anovulatory cycles, amenorrhoea and significant reduction in fertility. Nonetheless, dialysis patients do occasionally manage to conceive, and infertility cannot be assumed in patients with advanced CKD.

Accordingly, women at all stages of CKD who do not wish to conceive should be offered contraceptive advice. This advice is the same in CKD as for patients with normal kidney function. However, hypertension (if present) may limit the use of oestrogen-containing preparations.

The diagnosis of pregnancy may be difficult in women with advanced renal disease. Menstrual cycles are often erratic, leading to errors in timing the last menstrual period. Furthermore, serum beta-hCG levels may be raised due to impaired renal excretion, which can complicate interpretation of a standard pregnancy test.

Pregnancy in stage 1–3a CKD

There is little consistent evidence to suggest that women with early CKD lose renal function as a result of pregnancy, or have worse obstetric outcomes. A steady increase in glomerular filtration (and thus a reduction in serum creatinine) is generally observed as pregnancy progresses, as in individuals without CKD. Nonetheless, it is common for some women with mild CKD to show a transient deterioration in renal excretory function, often associated with hypertension, in the last trimester. In patients experiencing this effect, it is the severity of hypertension (rather than the extent of renal impairment) that has a lasting impact on renal survival. Accordingly, increased surveillance of blood pressure is advisable throughout pregnancy in people with pre-existing CKD at any stage, particularly in the last trimester. Readings should be maintained below 140/80 using the regimes applicable in pregnancy.

Women with proteinuric CKD should have checks of urine protein:creatinine ratio (PCR) at least monthly throughout pregnancy. Proteinuria from any cause often worsens during pregnancy due to increased glomerular filtration, and can sometimes reach nephrotic proportions (PCR>500mg/mmol) with hypoalbuminaemia. Angiotensin converting enzyme inhibitors (ACE-Is), which are useful in the management of proteinuria in the non-pregnant state, are contraindicated during pregnancy. Accordingly, meticulous blood pressure control, setting the target lower than usual (in the region of 120/70), is really all that can be offered to reduce protein excretion. It is advisable for pregnant women with heavy proteinuria to be placed under the joint care of a nephrologist and an obstetrician.

Pregnancy in stage 3b-4 CKD

About a third of pregnant women with CKD of this severity experience an accelerated rate of decline in renal function, which is irreversible. In patients who also have hypertension at the start of pregnancy, the risk of irreversible loss of renal function is even greater (about 50% of cases). The extent of renal decline is highly variable but about 10% of patients with CKD stage 3b–4, become dialysis-dependent at the end of their pregnancy. Obviously, the risk of this outcome is greater in those with worse renal excretory function at the start of pregnancy. Accordingly, women with an eGFR less than 45ml/minute should be counselled that pregnancy puts them at considerable risk of accelerating their renal decline towards end-stage disease.

Foetal outcomes from pregnancy in CKD

The effect of pre-existent CKD on the course and outcome of pregnancy has been studied in depth. Overall, the rate of live births is in fact only marginally less than in women with normal renal function and exceeds 90% when blood pressure is adequately controlled. However, this statistic belies some major risks, which make pregnancy more complicated, invasive and demanding of time and resources. As one might expect, the risks to the foetus are increased in the presence of more advanced maternal CKD.

The key point is that favourable foetal survival rates depend on the quality of blood pressure control even in the earliest stages of pregnancy. The risk of foetal death is approximately ten times higher in women with a mean arterial pressure greater than 105mmHg at conception, compared to those with adequate blood pressure control.

Whilst women with CKD are at significantly increased risk of pre-eclampsia, it is important to distinguish this syndrome from the co-existence of proteinuria with hypertension due to primary renal disease. In the latter case, proteinuria is detectable at the outset and throughout pregnancy. It has less impact on maternal and foetal outcomes than pre-eclampsia (which develops later in pregnancy).

The risk of prematurity and operative delivery is about six times greater in women with CKD (serum creatinine >125mmol/l) compared to the general population. The increased rate of pre-term delivery observed in women with CKD is largely related to intervention for pre-eclampsia and intrauterine growth retardation.

The risk to the foetus is not significantly affected by the aetiology of CKD, with the exception of lupus nephritis, which carries its own non-renal (immunologically mediated) risks in pregnancy.

Pregnancy counselling and advanced CKD

Women with advanced CKD need very careful counselling before embarking on a pregnancy. There is no degree of renal dysfunction at which pregnancy is contraindicated, but the risks both to mother and baby generally increase with more advanced CKD. Weighing the desire for a child against the risks of a pregnancy can be agonising for potential parents, and the responsibility of the healthcare professional is to ensure that their decision is fully informed by the facts. Referral of women with CKD to an appropriate specialist prior to conception is therefore strongly advised.

Key points

- Pregnancy in early CKD is low risk to mother and foetus, provided that blood pressure is meticulously monitored and controlled.

- Pregnancy in more advanced CKD risks loss of maternal renal function. The risk is greater, the more advanced the CKD.

- Foetal outcomes are generally favourable in CKD, but the risk of an operative delivery is higher.

- Pregnancy in the face of CKD requires careful counselling, which may best be provided by appropriate referral.

References and further reading

Williams, D. & Davison, J. (2008). Chronic kidney disease in pregnancy. *British Medical Journal.* **336**, 211–15.

16

Medicines management in CKD

The presence of CKD affects prescribing for two reasons: firstly, reduced excretion of drugs normally cleared by the kidney can lead to toxicity; and secondly, if the drug disturbs renal function, this may become clinically important when there is reduced renal reserve. Accordingly, it important to have a basic understanding of how the presence of CKD affects dosing schedules. It is not possible to describe in detail how each drug should be used in CKD in this short chapter. However, we can address the principles of pharmacology in CKD and identify the common drugs that present particular problems in patients with CKD.

Recent editions of the British National Formulary (BNF), which is ubiquitous and also available online (www.bnf.org), contain a paragraph in the dosing schedule giving advice on prescribing in renal impairment whenever renal function is relevant. Where this information is not sufficiently comprehensive, other useful reference sources include:

- The Summary of Product Characteristics (SPC), which provides more advice on dose reduction in renal impairment.
  The SPC is available electronically at www.emc.medicines.org.uk
- The Renal Drug Handbook (edited by C. Ashley & A. Currie). This comprehensive reference source is available both as a paperback and electronically. Most hospital pharmacy departments will hold this reference book and can use it to offer additional advice when needed.

The effects of CKD on drug excretion

In the past, dose recommendations in CKD were based on creatinine clearance (calculated from the Cockcroft and Gault formula). The BNF used rather vague terms such as 'moderate renal impairment' to draw attention to the need for caution in prescribing. More recently, the BNF has sought to harmonise its advice with current clinical practice by setting a limit of eGFR below which a drug should be used with caution or avoided. For most drugs in common use, the eGFR is a reasonable guide but some subjective adaptation of dose may still be required in patients who are at the extremes of body habitus.

The effect of drugs on CKD

Some drugs have a mechanism of action that will fairly reliably affect renal function (i.e. there is no idiosyncratic or allergic component to their renal effects). In individuals without CKD, their impact is not clinically apparent because of the capacity of the kidney to compensate. In CKD, in contrast, these drugs may have a profound effect because normal compensatory mechanisms are defective. Commonly encountered drugs that are particularly relevant in this context are:

- Non-steroidal anti-inflammatory drugs (NSAIDs) – causing usually reversible reduction in GFR
- Lithium – causing tubular toxicity
- Diuretics – causing dehydration and 'pre-renal' impairment
- Angiotensin converting enzyme inhibitors (ACE-Is) and Angiotensin II receptor antagonists (ARBs) – causing reduced renal perfusion in renovascular disease

The effect of these drugs on renal function is normally acute in onset (see Chapter 10) and usually reversible. However, harm may result if acute renal impairment is unrecognised and thus left untreated. Clinicians therefore need to know that these drugs can affect renal function and must increase the level of surveillance accordingly. As a guide, any patient with an eGFR less than 30ml/min in whom a potentially nephrotoxic drug is thought necessary should have a review of symptoms and renal function within two weeks of starting treatment.

CKD and common medicines

The remainder of this chapter will cover the common clinical situations where renal impairment presents a problem for the prescriber. The account is not comprehensive but addresses issues that are frequently encountered in general practice and often lead to queries being raised with nephrologists. If you encounter a problem when prescribing that is not adequately addressed here or in the reference sources, it is quite acceptable to request expert advice from a hospital pharmacist or the local nephrology team.

Anti-hypertensives

ACE-Is and ARBs

An ACE-I is the anti-hypertensive of choice in younger patients (under 55 years of age), those with diabetes and in patients with CKD and proteinuria. These drugs can decrease proteinuria and have a specific renoprotective effect, independent of their effect on blood pressure lowering, in patients with proteinuric CKD. The manner in which they should be used safely in CKD is described in depth in Chapter 9.

In patients with CKD, it is advisable to start ACE-Is and ARBs at a low dose and titrate upwards to the maximum dose or maximum tolerated dose over a period of four to six weeks. Renal function should be checked at initiation, one to two weeks after initiation, when dose titration is complete, and thereafter every six months. Starting with a low dose and titrating upwards slowly is particularly important in the elderly or those on diuretics, in whom hypotension may be less well tolerated. It is good practice to withhold diuretics for three to four days before starting an ACE-I or ARB in elderly patients with CKD, to avoid first-dose hypotension.

When patients are acutely unwell with nausea and vomiting or diarrhoea, they can quickly become dehydrated. If the patient continues to take regular ACE-Is or ARBs, reduced renal perfusion can result in severe acute renal impairment. These drugs should therefore be withheld if dehydration is a possibility.

Thiazide and thiazide-like diuretics

These agents inhibit the Na-Cl counter-transporter system in distal convoluted tubules. Because they rely on intact nephrons for their mode of action, they are less effective in CKD. In patients with an eGFR less than 30ml/min, loop diuretics are usually preferred. When fluid overload is a problem, metolazone is effective when combined with loop diuretics but requires careful monitoring of weight and renal function to avoid dehydration or hypokalaemia. This should normally be done with close guidance by the renal specialist team.

Loop diuretics

Furosemide and bumetanide act on the medullary part of the ascending limb of Henlé. In CKD, the kidneys become less responsive to their effects, but if the dosage is increased, they remain useful in managing hypertension and salt/water retention. In advanced kidney disease, the renal specialist may initiate high doses of loop diuretic (such as furosemide 250mg–1000mg daily).

Hypokalaemia is rarely a problem in CKD. Other electrolytes, notably calcium and magnesium, can become depleted after prolonged use of high-dose loop diuretics and levels should be checked periodically, especially if the patient becomes acutely unwell for any reason.

Potassium-sparing diuretics

In general the concomitant use of potassium-retaining diuretics such as amiloride or spironolactone should be avoided in CKD because of the risk of hyperkalaemia. However, spironolactone may be used in low doses for the treatment of heart failure. In patients with CKD, potassium levels must be monitored carefully, especially in combination with an ACE-I or ARB or during an episode of acute illness.

Calcium channel blockers (CCBs)

In general, calcium channel blockers should be introduced at the lowest starting dose and titrated upwards according to response. Ankle swelling is common with dihydropyridine CCBs (such as nifedipine and amlodipine) in CKD and must not be confused with fluid retention. In oedema due to CCBs, other symptoms and signs of salt/water retention (such as raised JVP, gallop rhythm and pulmonary congestion) are notably absent. Oedema often limits the use of CCBs in CKD.

Beta blockers

Atenolol and bisoprolol are renally excreted, and can therefore accumulate in CKD. Carvedilol and metoprolol are metabolised by the liver and are not dependent on renal function for elimination. In practice, this distinction is rarely a problem, but profound bradycardia in a CKD patient taking atenolol or bisoprolol should raise the possibility of drug toxicity. All beta blockers should be initiated at a low dose and titrated upwards according to pulse, blood pressure or side effects.

Alpha-receptor antagonists

In patients without CKD, alpha-receptor antagonists, such as doxazosin, are seen as a fourth-line drug option when trying to achieve target blood pressure. However, as dose adjustment is not necessary in CKD and they are safe to use in diabetes, these drugs are particularly useful for treating hypertension in CKD. Doses should be started low and titrated upwards according to response.

Antimicrobials

In the context of general practice, certain agents warrant particular attention. These are listed below.

Trimethoprim and co-trimoxozole

Trimethoprim is excreted by glomerular filtration and renal tubular secretion. Impaired renal function leads to delayed elimination and increased levels. Trimethoprim blocks the luminal sodium channels in the distal tubule, reducing potassium excretion (similar to amiloride). It also blocks tubular secretion of creatinine. The effect of trimethoprim is therefore to cause a rise in serum creatinine, which can be confused with an abrupt reduction in renal function (in fact, other toxic molecules are excreted normally). Because of this, trimethoprim and co-trimoxozole should be used with caution in CKD stage 4. Once the eGFR falls below 15ml/min, the dose should be reduced to half and renal function should be monitored closely.

Nitrofurantoin

Nitrofurantoin, which is commonly used for urinary tract infections, has its beneficial effect when concentrated in the urine. In patients with an eGFR below 60ml/min, this process is impaired and the drug therefore becomes less effective. It is contra-indicated in patients with a GFR below 50ml/min because of toxic accumulation and the risk of peripheral neuropathy.

Penicillins and cephalosporins

Most of these are excreted by the kidneys. Accordingly, lower doses or altered dosing schedules are required to avoid toxicity when eGFR falls below 15ml/min. The main manifestation of toxicity with oral penicillins or cephalosporins is a rash. High blood levels of ampicillin, amoxicillin and co-amoxiclav may cause crystalluria, particularly when used parenterally.

Macrolides

Macrolides, such as erythromycin and clarithromycin, can be administered in normal doses until the eGFR falls below 10ml/min. The main concern with the macrolides is the potential for drug interactions and increased risk of side effects associated with other concomitant medicines. Erythromycin and clarithromycin interact with anti-rejection drugs (such as ciclosporin A and tacrolimus), causing serious toxicity. If a macrolide is required, azithromycin is preferred in transplant patients.

Antivirals

Aciclovir accumulates in CKD and can cause serious neurotoxicity. When prescribing for patients with CKD stage 4–5, the BNF or SPC must be consulted for appropriate changes to the dosing schedule. The patient should be advised to stop treatment and seek medical advice if they become confused or start to hallucinate. It would be good practice to seek specialist advice from the renal team before prescribing oral antiviral drugs in patients with CKD stage 5 or on dialysis.

Tetracyclines

The only tetracyclines that are safe to use in patients with CKD stage 4–5 are doxycycline and minocycline. All others should be avoided because they may exacerbate renal failure.

Drugs used in diabetes

The pharmacology of hypoglycaemic agents in CKD is addressed in detail in Chapter 14.

Anti-inflammatory drugs

About 30% of patients with pre-existing CKD will develop worsening of function when given NSAIDs. NSAIDs may also cause hyperkalaemia, salt/water retention and hypertension. These effects are usually reversible when the NSAID is withdrawn.

NSAIDs inhibit cyclooxygenase (COX) and thereby reduce prostaglandin production within the kidney. Prostaglandins regulate intrarenal blood flow, and their inhibition causes a significant fall in glomerular filtration pressure in patients with CKD. This effect is greater in the presence of volume depletion (for example, dehydration or co-administration of diuretics) or when NSAIDs are used in combination with ACE-Is or ARBs. Maintenance of adequate renal function is particularly dependent on prostaglandin synthesis in the elderly, who are therefore especially susceptible to the renal effects of NSAIDs. COX-2 inhibitors confer no benefit over conventional NSAIDs in terms of renal effects.

As a general rule, NSAIDs should be avoided in CKD. Simple analgesics (such as paracetamol) should be used first line, especially during intercurrent illness when dehydration may occur (such as fever or diarrhoea). In cases of acute gout, colchicine is the preferred first-line treatment but where this is not tolerated, corticosteroids are an alternative.

In some individuals with CKD (for instance, those with chronic rheumatic diseases) a blanket ban on NSAIDs may have a profound effect on mobility and quality of life. In these circumstances, use of NSAIDs may be acceptable at the lowest effective dose, provided the risks and benefits have been adequately assessed and surveillance (notably of blood pressure, renal function and serum potassium level) is enhanced. The NSAIDs should be stopped if renal function declines markedly.

Aspirin can safely be used in low dose (75mg/day) for cardiovascular indications.

Opioid analgesics

Opioids are metabolised by the liver, but excretion of active metabolites may depend on kidney function. Starting doses of codeine, dihydrocodeine, and tramadol should therefore be reduced. Fixed-dose combination products should be avoided where possible.

Morphine accumulates in patients with CKD stage 4–5 due to reduced and variable renal excretion of active metabolites. Short-acting preparations should be used in the first instance and titrated according to response and side effects. Dosing intervals should be longer than normal (for example, six-hourly rather than four-hourly). Oxycodone is often preferred as first-line treatment for acute pain relief in CKD since it has no clinically important active metabolites. Oxycodone orally is about 1.5 to 2 times more potent than morphine, and is excreted via the kidneys.

Fentanyl and buprenorphine are both metabolised in the liver, making them a useful alternative to consider for chronic pain management in patients with CKD. They are not suitable for acute pain because opioids delivered via a transdermal patch take over 24 hours to reach steady state in CKD.

Low molecular weight heparins (LMWHs)

Increasingly, subcutaneous LMWHs are being administered in the community as prophylaxis against, or treatment for, thromboembolic disease. Elimination of these molecules is almost entirely renal, and people with CKD are therefore at risk of haemorrhagic complications. Although specific guidance varies between institutions, it is generally the case that patients with an eGFR less than 30ml/min in which LMWH treatment is necessary should receive half the standard dose. It is also recommended that factor Xa should be monitored weekly during treatment, which makes using these agents in advanced CKD clinically cumbersome and expensive. For this reason, use of unfractionated heparin, which can be monitored using relatively inexpensive laboratory tests, is often preferred in CKD until adequate warfarinisation is achieved. In the absence of national guidelines, one can only refer to the locally implemented policy regarding management of thromboembolic disease in CKD.

Bisphosphonates

The use of these agents in CKD is discussed in Chapter 11 in the context of renal bone disease.

Lipid-lowering drugs

There is an increased risk of myositis when statins are used in patients with an eGFR less than 30ml/min. Accordingly, statin treatment should be initiated at a lower dosage than usual in CKD. In advanced CKD (stage 4–5) doses of simvastatin over 10mg per day should be avoided. Atrovastatin can be safely used as an alternative, or the simvastatin can be supplemented with ezetemibe.

Statins interact with ciclosporin, leading to toxicity. This effect is reduced with pravastatin, which is therefore preferred when a statin is required for a transplant recipient. CKD also increases the risk of myositis associated with fibrates. Accordingly, all fibrates should be used with caution in CKD (eGFR<60ml/min) and modified-release preparations should be avoided in patients with an eGFR lower than 30ml/min.

Vaccinations

The Department of Health (DOH) recommends that patients who have CKD or have a transplanted kidney have an annual influenza vaccination and pneumovax if appropriate.

Many renal units are now following the DOH guidance on minimising infection by blood-borne viruses. They may advise hepatitis B vaccination for patients with CKD stage 4–5 who are likely to require dialysis or be transplanted. The high-dose (40mcg) injection is required in these patients because of their impaired immune response.

Key points

- Although the presence of renal impairment affects prescribing for a large number of drugs, the BNF now contains clear advice on how CKD should affect prescription.
- The presence of CKD increases the clinical impact of drug nephrotoxicity. Clinicians have to know how to prescribe drugs in which this is particularly important (NSAIDs, ACE-Is and ARBs, lithium and diuretics).

References and further reading

Ashley, C. & Currie, A. (2008). The Renal Drug Handbook. Oxford: Radcliffe Publishing Ltd.Online edition: www.radcliffe-oxford.com/electronic/E24_Renal_Drug_Handbook_3e_%28online%29/default.asp

British National Formulary. (2006). The patient, the drug and the kidney. *Drug and Therapeutic Bulletin*. **44** (12), 89–95.

British National Formulary. (2012). BMJ Group and Pharmaceutical Press. www.bnf.org

BNF is distributed free to all NHS hospitals and GPs by the Department of Health. It is published annually by the BMJ Group, Tavistock Square, London WC1H 9JP and Pharmaceutical Press, 1 Lambeth High Street London SE1 7JN.

Galbraith, A., Bullock, S., Manias, E., Hunt, B. & Richards, A. *The Fundamentals of Pharmacology: An Applied Approach for Nursing and Health*. 2nd edition. Pearson Education.

Rang, H.P. & Dale, M.M. (2007). *Pharmacology*. 6th edition. Philadelphia, US: Churchill Livingstone.

17

When all else fails: Management of end-stage kidney disease

Although CKD is thought to affect about 10% of the population, it is quite unusual for a patient with this condition to progress to the point where they require dialysis. As we have seen in earlier chapters, much management of CKD is aimed at reducing death from cardiovascular disease rather than preventing end-stage kidney disease. Nonetheless, about 100 people per million of the population commence dialysis in the UK every year, with the number of patients on dialysis increasing by about 8% per annum. Most GP practices currently have three or four patients on their register who have a transplant or require dialysis, and this is likely to increase in future.

The rise in dialysis population is fuelled by several factors, such as the increasing incidence of hypertension and diabetes and success in reducing other causes of death. But the most important factor has been the increased readiness of dialysis programmes to offer treatment to older people with multiple co-morbidities who might not have been considered suitable in the past. The average age of a dialysis patient increases annually in the UK and is currently 65.5 years. The acceptance rate onto dialysis is highest in those aged 75–79 years.

At what stage is primary care-based management of CKD insufficient?

It is quite acceptable for patients with CKD stage 1–3b to be managed in a primary care setting for years. However, at stage 4 CKD, they should generally be referred to a specialist centre. Nowadays, most patients warrant specialist assessment, and they should all be given the opportunity to make an informed choice about what they want to do when their kidneys finally fail. Referral to the renal unit at this stage of CKD is not necessarily a request for dialysis work-up, but a request for expert assessment and the instigation of appropriate therapy – which may be dialysis but may sometimes be restricted to anaemia management, non-dialytic symptom control or end-of-life care.

In the renal unit, people with stage 4 CKD who are expected to progress to stage 5 CKD are usually managed in a specific 'low-clearance' clinic – the name refers to low clearance of renal toxins and their consequent accumulation in the blood. In this clinic, they are prepared for future dialysis with education about the various ways in which life can be sustained once the kidneys fail. Once they are fully acquainted with the options open to them, they are encouraged to make an informed choice as to the treatment they wish to receive. They must do this well in advance of end-stage kidney failure, since some modalities need preparation in advance (for example, creation of an arteriovenous fistula for haemodialysis). By formulating a plan prospectively, patients suffer fewer complications and have less morbidity when treatment is ultimately instigated.

The main choices open to people with end-stage disease are to have a renal transplant, to commence haemodialysis, to commence peritoneal dialysis or to opt for conservative (non-dialytic) therapy. Within these broad options there are further choices to be made, which depend on the patient's individual circumstances and wishes. Although a non-specialist is unlikely to be involved in guiding a patient through the process of planning renal replacement therapy, you may encounter patients with earlier stages of CKD who may enquire about their future. Accordingly, it is worth having some basic knowledge about the options available and their suitability for particular types of individual.

The best treatment for renal failure is a pre-emptive (i.e. just before end-stage disease), well-matched transplant from a living donor. If no such donor is available, a deceased donor transplant is the next-best option. The renal team aim to establish people on the transplant list when their eGFR falls below 15mls/min or they are thought to be within six months of end-stage disease. If a pre-emptive transplant is available, dialysis can be avoided altogether. Because a donor is not usually immediately forthcoming, most patients who receive a transplant do so after a period of dialysis.

Not all patients are suitable for transplantation and a thorough analysis of potential risks and benefits is required before they are placed on the waiting list. A key consideration is the patient's cardiovascular health. This is because the commonest cause of kidney transplant failure is death of the recipient (with a functioning kidney) due to heart disease. A past history of cancer does not preclude transplantation, but the chance of recurrence when on immunosuppression needs to be assessed. Transplantation can usually be considered when a patient has been in remission for a certain length of time, which depends on the type of cancer in question.

Very occasionally, patients may express the wish to be considered for transplantation even though they understand that the risks are great. Ultimately, the decision to transplant lies with the transplanting unit; whilst patient choice is important, transplantable kidneys are a limited national resource and transplant units have a duty to ensure they are used to the greatest positive effect.

Once accepted as a possible transplant recipient, the patient has a number of different ways of receiving a new kidney. The success rate of all methods is high, although living donor transplants yield the best results (see Table 17.1). Note that the data shows ten year survival for kidneys which were (obviously) transplanted ten years ago, using techniques and drugs prevalent at that time. It may be that a higher proportion of kidney transplants undertaken today will still be functioning ten years hence.

Table 17.1 *Survival of kidney transplants from 3 months to 10 years. Note that a greater percentage of living transplants survive at each time interval compared to deceased donor transplants. (Data from OPTN/SRTR annual report for transplants undertaken between 2000 and 2008).*

	3 months	1 year	5 years	10 years
Deceased donor transplant	96.1%	93.0%	72.5%	44.6%
Living donor transplant	97.9%	96.4%	82.5%	59.6%

Cadaveric transplants are of two types.

- **Donation after brain death (DBD):** Organs are removed when a ventilated patient on an intensive care unit meets the strict standardised criteria for brain death and consent is obtained from the donor's family. Simultaneous kidney-pancreas transplants (see Chapter 14) are all of this type.

- **Donation after cardiac death (DCD):** Cardio-respiratory support is withdrawn prior to the retrieval operation. This may occur because relatives find it hard to accept the death of a loved one by brain death criteria alone and wish to be present during cardio-respiratory arrest.

There is a higher risk of ischaemic injury to DCD transplants, so they are managed differently when transplanted. However, ultimate outcomes are broadly similar. Organs are allocated to recipients according to a nationally-controlled scoring system which uses, amongst other criteria, the immunological match, age match, waiting time of a potential recipient etc. to establish the most suitable recipient. It goes without saying that there are not enough donated organs to meet demand and some patients wait for years for an offer of transplantation.

Living donation is the method of choice but is limited by the availability of suitable living donors. In recent years various ways have been found to enable living donation where previously it was not thought possible. The types of living donation are as follows:-

- **Direct living donation (LD):** This is the standard donation of a kidney from a willing donor to a recipient who may or may not be related. The Human Tissue Authority needs to establish that there is a relationship of a suitable kind (e.g. a longstanding close friend) before allowing the transplant to proceed. Nowadays, blood group incompatibility does not always preclude living transplant, although such transplants are available only in highly specialised centres.

- **Paired living donation:** Where a willing donor is immunologically incompatible with their intended recipient, other donor-recipient pairs in a similar position are sought. If the donors in each pair are suitable for the other pair's recipient, the kidneys can be swapped between them.

- **Pooled living transplant:** This is, in effect, an extension of the paired scheme whereby there is a three-way (or even more) swap between donor-recipient pairs in which the donor of each pair is immunologically incompatible with their recipient.

- **Altruistic donation:** The Human Tissue Act of 2007 for the first time allowed individuals, motivated entirely by altruism, to donate a kidney to recipients with whom they have no relationship. This is usually 'non-directed' – i.e. the donor has no influence over the choice of recipient and the donated kidney is allocated in the same way as from a deceased donor. However, directed altruistic donation is not illegal and it is likely that there will be more people coming forward to donate to people who they do not know personally, but whose circumstances have induced them to want to donate. The ethics of this is open to debate. Which patients will pull on the heart-strings and which will not? Will potential recipients advertise on line for a donor? This is already happening.

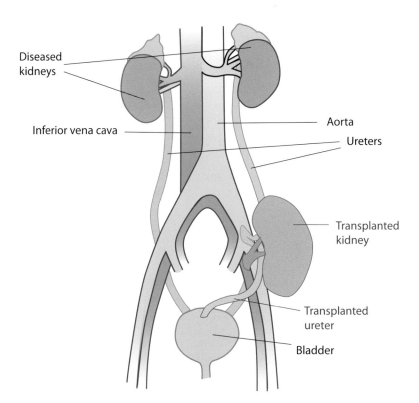

Figure 17.1 *Renal transplantation. The donor kidney is anastomosed to the donor iliac vessels and the bladder. The diseased native kidneys are left in situ.*

No matter how the donated kidneys are obtained, the transplant operation is broadly similar. An incision about 15cm long is made in one or other iliac fossa. The donor kidney vessels are anastomosed to the internal iliac vessels and the donor ureter is inserted into the bladder. The recipient's own renal tissue is left in situ (see Figure 17.1). Often the transplanted kidney produces urine as soon as the clamps are removed from the blood vessels and then develops a brisk diuresis over the next few days, requiring careful postoperative fluid management. On other occasions, the function of the transplanted kidney develops gradually after a sluggish start. Transplant recipients usually stay in hospital for about a week and then have very frequent reviews in a specialist transplant clinic – at least twice weekly initially. The aim, which is usually achieved, is for the serum creatinine to lie within the normal range after three months.

Immunosuppression

Standard regimes use calcineurin antagonists (ciclosporin A or tacrolimus) combined with a drug to interfere with lymphocyte function (e.g. mycophenolate mofetil) and, in the first few months after transplantation, corticosteroids. These drugs are usually prescribed in a shared care arrangement with primary care. The common side effects are:

- **Calcineurin antagonists:** hirsutism (especially ciclosporin A), tremor (especially tacrolimus), gum hypertrophy and post-transplant diabetes. These agents do not often cause bone marrow suppression.

- **Mycophenolate:** leucopaenia or other manifestations of bone marrow suppression, diarrhoea or other gastrointestinal symptoms. Both these effects are dose-dependent.

All immunosuppressive agents contribute to an increase in the long-term risk of cancer. Non-melanotic skin cancer (squamous or basal cell) is particularly prevalent and all transplant recipients are counselled not to expose themselves to the sun. Many transplant units organise regular specialist skin surveillance. Amongst the other malignancies, one that is worthy of mention is a particular type of Epstein-Barr Virus-driven lymphoma (Post-Transplant Lymphoproliferative Disease or PTLD). Its identification and differentiation from 'standard' lymphoma are important because it may resolve completely on reduction of immunosuppression.

Opportunistic infections are most prevalent during the first year post-transplant. Cytomegalovirus is particularly troublesome during this time and at-risk individuals receive anti-viral prophylaxis. Cotrimoxozole prophylaxis against pneumocystis pneumonia is required during the first six months. As the transplant settles in, immunosuppression can be gradually reduced and the risk of serious opportunistic infection diminishes, although viral warts may become a particular problem in the long term, warranting repeated removal.

Haemodialysis (HD)

This is a process whereby the patient's circulation is connected to an extracorporeal circuit and pumped through a dialyser, where it runs in close proximity to a specially prepared solution (dialysate), separated by a specially designed semi-permeable membrane. By diffusion, toxins from the blood cross into the dialysate, which is disposed of, whilst the blood is returned to the patient via the circuit. The circulation of blood through the dialyser continues for several hours and the toxin concentration gradually falls to safe (but not normal) levels. The haemodialysis machine is in effect a computer-assisted pump that meticulously regulates the rate of blood flow, the rate of dialysis flow and the amount of unwanted fluid removed from the patient.

To obtain adequate flow through the extracorporeal circuit, it is necessary to access a large blood vessel with large-bore needles. It is not feasible to repeatedly access the arterial or deep vein circulation. This problem is overcome by undertaking an operation to divert arterial blood into a superficial vein – an arteriovenous fistula (see Figure 17.2).

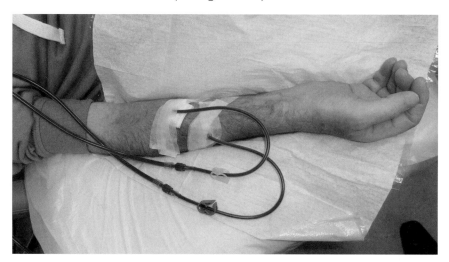

Figure 17.2 *An arteriovenous fistula being used for haemodialysis. Blood at arterial pressure leaves the circulation via the proximal needle. It is pumped through the dialysis machine and then returned to the circulation via the distal needle. (Photograph © Robert Lewis)*

The fistula cannot be used immediately as the vein needs to mature and 'arterialise' before it is suitable to accept the dialysis needles. This is why haemodialysis needs to be planned about six months before it is needed. Patients who present too late can be dialysed temporarily via in-dwelling jugular catheters, but these provide inefficient dialysis and are prone to infection. Mortality and morbidity are increased in patients presenting with end-stage kidney disease in whom there has been no prior preparation. Renal units are subject to national comparative audit, and the proportion of haemodialysis patients undergoing their first treatment through a functioning fistula is one marker of the quality of care a unit provides.

In the UK, haemodialysis costs about £30,000 per annum, not including other ancillary costs such as patient transport, hospital admissions and erythropoietin therapy. Traditionally, patients receive thrice-weekly sessions each lasting four hours – this being a reasonable balance between the amount of solute clearance required to maintain health and the healthcare resources available. However, within this traditional dialysis regime, there are choices, which are listed below.

Centre-based haemodialysis

The patient attends the main renal unit three times a week, where dialysis nurses undertake the treatment. The dialysis unit is usually within the hospital, so specialist medical staff are available. This modality is best suited to people with significant co-morbidities, which might make their dialysis more difficult or unstable. However, it is the most expensive way to deliver dialysis.

Satellite-based haemodialysis

The patient attends a unit away from the main hospital where nurses undertake the dialysis (see Figure 17.3). Many of these units are set up and staffed by private companies who are contracted by the NHS to provide dialysis at a negotiated cost per treatment. However, the patients remain under the supervision of NHS consultants from the commissioning renal unit. Patients on standard thrice-weekly haemodialysis can have holidays if they are sufficiently stable to be safely accommodated at a satellite unit near their chosen destination.

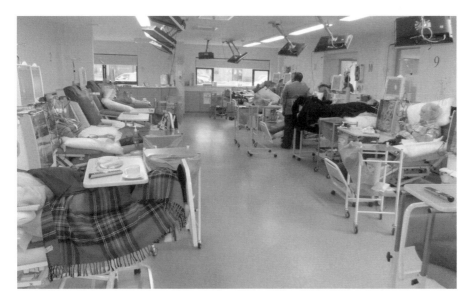

Figure 17.3 *A typical satellite dialysis unit – in this case, on an industrial estate. Patients are allocated a station at a set time, which they must attend three times a week. Nursing staff set up the machines and insert the needles, but staffing is maintained at levels suitable for stable, low-dependency patients. Patients with more co-morbidities are better suited to dialysis in a hospital, where specialist intervention is available when needed. (Photograph © Robert Lewis)*

Home haemodialysis

This modality was popular during the early years of haemodialysis but declined as satellite facilities expanded. In recent years, it has been appreciated that more frequent dialysis results in better long-term outcomes than traditional thrice-weekly treatments. As such frequent treatments are best delivered in the patient's home, there has been a resurgence of interest in home therapy. New technology has produced small dialysis machines that can easily be used six days a week within the home without re-plumbing the domestic water supply (see Figure 17.4). The main limitation of this technique is the patients themselves – the assessment team must be reassured that the physical, intellectual and psychosocial requirements of home therapy are attainable. The patient also needs to have someone available in the home during the dialysis sessions in case complications occur.

Figure 17.4 *An example of the new generation of home haemodialysis machines. These can be conveniently accommodated within the home without any alteration to the domestic water supply. The patient usually requires about three hours of dialysis, six days a week, which can be undertaken in the living room in front of the TV. (Photograph © Nxstage Medical Inc)*

Peritoneal dialysis (PD)

By introducing a carefully constituted, sterile solution into the peritoneal cavity through an in-dwelling catheter, and leaving it in contact with the highly vascular peritoneal membrane, toxins can be dialysed from the blood along concentration gradients. Regular refreshment of the dialysate maintains these gradients, ensuring adequate solute clearance. The amount of fluid removed during dialysis is controlled by varying the osmotic gradient between blood and dialysate. This variation is achieved by supplying the patients with dialysate solutions that contain different concentrations of glucose and instructing them on which solution to use to maintain a target weight, which is prescribed on the basis of clinical signs of volume overload or depletion.

PD has the advantage of allowing patients to dialyse themselves at home and to have greater control over their own lives. They need sufficient storage space for the boxes of dialysate, which are delivered by the manufacturing company. The great danger of PD is peritonitis, caused by inadvertent introduction of bacteria into the peritoneal cavity during an exchange. For this reason, meticulous sterile technique needs to be ensured. There are three ways in which PD can be undertaken, as described below.

Continuous ambulatory PD (CAPD)

With this technique, a patient instills (usually) 2 litres of dialysate into their peritoneal cavity four times a day, giving a dwell time of approximately six hours. During the dwell, they can go about their usual daily tasks, but they have to find somewhere clean and calm to undertake a dialysate exchange, which takes 20–30 minutes. The used dialysate can be discarded into a toilet, and the used dialysate bags are packed away for subsequent collection and incineration. Some patients find standard CAPD wearing, as they never have a day away from a regimented timetable of exchanges. However, they can take dialysate with them for short breaks or even have deliveries arranged at holiday destinations, which gives them a degree of freedom. Some patients have successfully dialysed with CAPD for over 15 years.

Automated PD (APD)

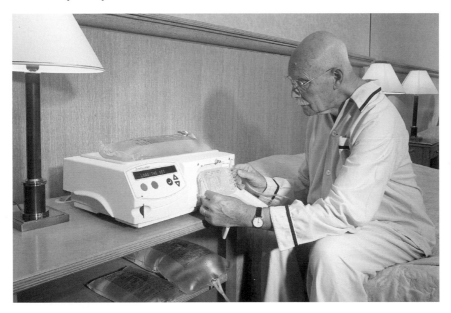

Figure 17.5 *An automated peritoneal dialysis machine primed for use at the bedside. Note the bag of dialysate sitting on the warmer on top of the machine. The contents of this bag are infused into the patient's peritoneal cavity and replaced by fresh dialysate, which is then warmed in anticipation of the next exchange. Dialysis effluent drains out of the patient into other bags, which are discarded in the morning. In total, about 12 litres of dialysate are infused and exchanged throughout the night. The whole process is controlled by an electronically programmed cassette, which the patient is inserting into the machine. (Photograph © Baxter Ltd)*

With this technique, the patient is supplied with a bedside machine that regulates the inflow and outflow of dialysate (see Figure 17.5). The required number of bags of dialysate is attached to the machine before retiring. At bedtime, the patient attaches the in-dwelling dialysis catheter to the machine, turns out the light and goes to sleep. Dialysis exchanges then take place automatically throughout the night. During the day, the patient is freed from the need for repeated exchanges, although it is usual to leave a bag of dialysate in the abdomen throughout the day to add to the efficiency of the technique.

Assisted PD

When the patient is infirm and cannot undertake dialysate exchanges, this need not preclude PD. Family members or carers can be trained to undertake the exchanges (either CAPD or APD) on their behalf. In addition, dialysis companies provide assisted PD through their own trained nursing staff for patients who do not have adequate support in their homes. The nurses can attend the patient to set up and start APD, returning at a later time to disconnect the machine. Because of the requirement for additional input from nurses, assisted PD is more expensive than conventional PD, and this has limited the adoption of assisted PD in some parts of the country.

Conservative care

It is important to distinguish between conservative care and palliative or end-of-life care; the latter is addressed in depth in the next chapter. Conservative care is an active treatment that aims to extend and improve the quality of life. It is particularly applicable to the elderly who may not wish to spend their last years being troubled by dialysis. Treatment focuses on slowing progression of CKD (see Chapter 9), management of anaemia and symptom control by the methods described in the following chapter.

There is good evidence to show that dialysis and conservative care can extend lifespan to the same extent in people over the age of 80 years with end-stage kidney disease. One might therefore reasonably ask why dialysis is offered to the very elderly at all. The problem is that health ('biological age') is highly variable and subjective; one cannot predict with any exactitude how individual elderly kidney patients will tolerate dialysis. Accordingly, there is a tendency to 'give them a try'– every dialysis unit has a 90-year-old who has been on dialysis for several years and has coped better than anyone could have predicted.

Deciding when end-stage kidney disease has been reached

Having made a plan about the treatment options they favour when they reach end-stage kidney disease, patients with CKD can be monitored closely in the low clearance clinic for months or even years. But what defines the point at which the plan should be put into action?

Because CKD usually progresses gradually, deciding when 'end-stage disease' has been reached is a matter of judgement. Blood tests are useful, but should not be the only criteria considered. Most nephrologists would agree that it is unsafe to leave a patient without treatment if they exhibit:

- Persistent acidosis where the serum bicarbonate is less than 12mmol/l despite treatment with bicarbonate tablets
- Persistent hyperkalaemia (potassium>6mmol/l) that does not improve with dietary restriction or adaptation of drug regime
- eGFR persistently less than 7ml/min

Symptoms may be useful in indicating the onset of end-stage disease. They may arise from the build-up of toxins (lassitude, anorexia, nausea or vomiting) or salt/water overload (shortness of breath, orthopnoea or oedema). These symptoms develop gradually and patients often learn to accommodate them rather than accept the need for dialysis. Only after dialysis is established do they retrospectively appreciate how the symptoms crept up on them.

As neither blood tests nor symptoms give a definitive threshold for a diagnosis of end-stage disease, the clinician has to weigh up the danger of leaving a patient without treatment against the negative impact dialysis will have on lifestyle, employment, holiday plans and other aspects. Nephrologists tend to rely on their own experience when advising on the best course of action.

Outcomes from renal replacement therapy: What can patients expect?

Before the advent of renal replacement therapy, end-stage renal disease was effectively a death sentence. During the early decades of dialysis, the best that could be offered was the deferment of death – and some of us remember sallow, broken-looking individuals limping towards dialysis units in the 1980s. But, with improving dialysis technology, the introduction of erythropoietin and effective prevention of bone disease, life – and, importantly, quality of life – for patients with renal failure can be sustained. The principles of patient education and patient choice, coupled with efforts to design renal replacement therapies around the needs of the individual, have led to good outcomes.

In younger patients, dialysis should be viewed as a holding measure whilst awaiting transplantation or as a stop-gap between a failed transplant and a subsequent graft. In those unsuitable for transplantation, dialysis offers a good quality of life to the majority. In fact, many elderly patients express great satisfaction with the social interaction provided by the dialysis unit ('It's our Darby and Joan Club!'). Dialysis of either type can be continued for many years if necessary – some haemodialysis patients have remained on that treatment for three decades with a reasonable quality of life.

Where transplantation is feasible, a return to nearly normal quality of life should be expected – including all sorts of sports (Jonah Lomu, the New Zealand All Black rugby player being a good example), normal fertility and only a few employment restrictions. Of course, such an outcome cannot be guaranteed: there are still risks of rejection, infection and surgical complications, and patients are informed about the possibility of these in the course of preparation for transplant. Nonetheless, modern immunosuppressive regimes are well tolerated and highly effective. In particular, the long-term effects of high-dose steroids are a thing of the past.

The most common cause of death in dialysis patients is cardiovascular disease. Although CKD predisposes to atherosclerotic disease, the cardiovascular disease of dialysis patients is also characterised by disseminated vascular calcification (the result of mineral bone disease – see Chapter 11) and myocardial fibrosis. Sudden cardiac death, presumably as a result of arrhythmia caused by fibrosis of the conducting system, is particularly common in dialysis patients. Figure 17.6 shows the increased prevalence of cardiovascular disease in the dialysis population of all ages, compared to normal.

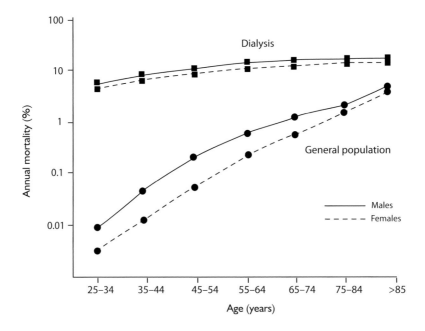

Figure 17.6 *Cardiovascular mortality compared to the general population of people in different age ranges receiving haemodialysis. Note that the annual cardiovascular mortality rate of dialysis patients in the age range 25–34 is the same as that for people aged over 85 in the general population. (Adapted from Foley et al., 1998)*

Mortality is improved if dialysis patients receive a transplant. This is another reason why patients with advanced CKD should be transplanted where this is feasible. Nonetheless, cardiovascular disease remains a major problem in transplant recipients; and some of the drugs used for immunosuppression add to the cardiovascular risk already accumulated after years of CKD. The causes of death in dialysis and transplant patients are compared in Figure 17.7.

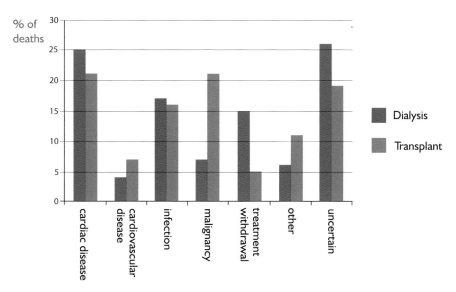

Figure 17.7 *Causes of death for patients on dialysis (n = 1379) and those with a transplant (n = 189) in UK 2009. (Based on Renal Registry, 13th Annual Report)*

Key points

- End-stage renal disease has a number of treatment solutions that can be tailored to the requirements of the individual to give a good quality of life.

- Assessment by the renal unit is useful, even in those patients for whom the options of dialysis or transplantation are undesirable or unfeasible. Well-configured conservative care under the direction of a renal unit can optimise quality of life in people with co-morbidities.

- Pre-emptive living donor transplant offers the best outcomes and should be regarded as the option of choice in most cases of end-stage renal disease.

References and further reading

Caskey, F., Dawnay, A., Farrington, K. et al. (2011). UK Renal Registry 2010: 13th Annual Report of the Renal Registry. *Nephron Clinical Practice*. **119** (2).

Foley, R.N., Parfrey, P.S. & Sarnak, M.J. (1998). Clinical epidemiology of cardiovascular disease in chronic renal disease. *American Journal of Kidney Disease*. **32**, S112–S119.

NHS Blood and Transplant centre-specific reports

www.organdonation.nhs.uk/ukt/statistics/centre-specific_reports/kidney_centre-specific_reports.jsp

NHS Choices: dialysis www.nhs.uk/conditions/dialysis/pages/introduction.aspx

Stein, A. & Wild, J. (2002). *Kidney Failure Explained.* London: Class Publishing.

OPTN/SRTR Annual report (2010). Transplant data 2000–2009 http://www.srtr.org/annual_reports/2010/default.htm

18

Symptom control and end-of-life care in CKD

This chapter deals with the particular needs of patients with stage 5 CKD as they enter the terminal phase of their disease – either because they have declined an offer of dialysis or have decided to withdraw from it. Primary care teams are likely to become involved at this stage because many patients prefer to die at home or in a local hospice rather than in the renal unit in which they have formerly received their specialist care.

Although palliative care programmes have traditionally focused on supporting people with cancer, the need for something similar for people with end-stage CKD is now well recognised. The National Service Framework for Renal Services (2005) included a section on end-of-life care, which focused on the need to expand integrated palliative care services for people with CKD. This has been accomplished in most areas of the UK.

As the number of older people approaching end-stage CKD increases, it has become clear that offering dialysis to some patients does not prolong their life and, in some instances, contributes to a significant deterioration in the quality of life of their last months. Once informed of this fact during the 'low clearance' education which they receive at the renal unit, many elderly or infirm patients will opt for conservative treatment (see Chapter 17). This may keep them well for months or even years, but ultimately, as uraemic toxins and fluid build up, they are likely to develop troublesome symptoms. The onset is often insidious and patients should regularly be asked to review their chosen treatment option to ensure they are happy to continue with a conservative plan – they must be reassured that they are allowed to change their minds and accept dialysis. If conservative care continues, they will eventually decline to a point where end-of-life measures need to be put into place to ensure that they pass away without distress, pain or fear.

Another instance where end-of-life care becomes relevant is when patients on dialysis decide to withdraw from further treatment. They may do this because they have reached the point, either through age or comorbidity, when they consider the rigours of dialysis too burdensome. This is a brave decision because dialysis patients (by definition) have negligible renal function and can therefore be expected to die within a few days of withdrawal. One must be sure that the patient is expressing an informed decision and that it is shared with relatives or other loved ones. Involvement of the family ensures that a frank discussion can then be had about end-of-life preferences – there is little value in a patient expressing the wish to die at home if the family does not support that decision.

Planning end-of-life care

In CKD, the need to develop an end-of-life care plan rarely comes out of the blue. Decisions to opt for conservative care or to withdraw from dialysis are made by the patient with due consideration over a period of time. There is therefore no good reason why professionals should not initiate plans to meet their requirements weeks before the time of death. Nonetheless, one still encounters patients with CKD which has been known about for years, who opt for conservative treatment but who are admitted via the A&E department in extremis in their last days with no end-of-life plan in place. In many cases, this is due to poor communication between primary and secondary care. Often, everyone involved has avoided asking the key question 'When the time comes, where would you like to die?'

From what is known about patient preference, but also taking into account the pressures on in-patient beds and public finance, patients dying of kidney failure should be managed in the community where this is possible. Primary care teams are usually at the hub of the various agencies which will be involved. Patients should all have care plans which should include details of the professionals who are involved in their care delivery, triggers for review and named people to contact for advice and support. Although care plans are held by patients, other services, such as community palliative care teams and out-of-hours services, will need to be aware of them. Some renal units have nursing staff specifically trained in delivery of palliative care in kidney disease, who may liaise with primary care teams and offer specialist advice.

There have been a number of national initiatives aimed at optimising end-of-life care. The most well-known is the Liverpool Care Pathway from the Marie Curie Palliative Care Institute, which has recently (2008) been updated under the auspices of the Department of Health to provide a pathway of care and drug therapy specific to the needs of patients dying of end-stage renal failure.

Symptom management

In patients accepting renal replacement therapy, the symptoms of end-stage kidney disease are signals that dialysis should be initiated. By removing uraemic toxins, dialysis usually brings relief. This course of action is clearly not applicable to patients opting for conservative care. Nonetheless, symptoms can be effectively controlled by other means which will now be described. The suitability of a given remedy is determined by the proximity of the patient to death from uraemia; long-term oral medication might be the best option for early symptoms in a patient receiving active conservative management, whereas stronger parenteral treatment may be more appropriate for a patient who has opted to withdraw from dialysis and has a very limited prognosis.

Pain

Pain experienced by patients with stage 5 CKD is often caused by co-morbidities rather than the renal disease itself. Common causes are ischaemic pain from peripheral vascular disease, neuropathic pain (often related to diabetes) and bone pain from osteoporosis or renal bone disease. In patients having conservative care, NSAIDs should be avoided as they may precipitate renal failure and thus shorten life.

The World Health Organisation (WHO) analgesic ladder approach to managing pain should be used, using drugs suitable in patients with severe renal impairment. This is summarised in Table 18.1

Table 18.1 *A summary of pain relief for people with stage 5 CKD.*

Step 1	Paracetamol 1g qds
Step 2	Tramadol 50-100mg qds (avoid codeine, dihydrocodeine)
Step 3	Moderate pain: Fentanyl is the safest drug to use in stage 5 CKD (by patch, if out of hospital). Oxycodone or buprenorphine are alternatives Severe pain: Fentanyl (25 mcg starting dose) subcutaneously (s/c) as required, then in a continuous subcutaneous infusion if necessary.

Pruritus

Uraemic pruritus is a common problem for people with renal disease but the evidence supporting pharmacological treatments is limited. It can be very distressing and is difficult to abolish completely. Management should include:

- Exclusion of other causes of pruritus, including systemic or dermatological causes
- Correction of high blood phosphate (using phosphate binders, see Chapter 11) and anaemia (I.V. iron or erythropoietin if necessary)
- Liberal use of emollients including bath additives. Some emollients contain antipruritic additives such as urea and lauromacrogols
- If pruritus is widespread, terfenadine may be used, or if sedation is required (as it often is), chlorpheniramine
- Ondansetron can sometimes be effective as a last resort.

Fluid overload

Fluid overload is to be expected as the capacity for the kidneys to handle salt and water declines. Fluid restriction is an obvious intervention but should not be imposed to the extent that thirst becomes intrusive. At least a litre a day should be allowed. Sucking ice cubes is a good way to ease thirst without excessive fluid intake.

As fluid builds up, patients may experience dyspnoea or orthopnoea due to pulmonary oedema. This can be treated as follows:

- Oral furosemide titrated to doses up to 480mg.
- Metolazone 5mg per day may be added in severe cases – this can sometimes enhance the effects of loop diuretics.
- Where feasible, furosemide can be more effective as an intravenous infusion.
- Infusion of glyceryl trinitrate offloads the pulmonary circulation and reduces pulmonary oedema. It is best reserved for acute pulmonary oedema causing distress.
- Where patients are being nursed in the community and intravenous infusions are not feasible or desirable, the distress of pulmonary oedema should be relieved with opiates such as fentanyl or diamorphine s/c in doses sufficient to bring relief.

Nausea, vomiting and anorexia

Nausea and vomiting are very common symptoms in advanced renal failure. All the conventional anti-emetics are applicable in whatever dose is required to improve symptoms, including ondasetron if necessary.

Nausea and vomiting can be improved with modification of the diet. Patients often express a dislike for high-protein foods, possibly because these contribute to the production of uraemic toxins. Accordingly, high calorie foods should be favoured. It is not unusual for patients at end-stage renal failure to develop a new liking for sweet puddings which they have always detested in the past. Not infrequently, patients complain of an unpleasant metallic taste in their mouths. This may be helped with mouthwashes etc., but there is also some evidence that oral zinc supplementation can be useful.

Insomnia

Sleep disturbance is almost universal in patients with end-stage renal failure, most notably loss of diurnal rhythm; patients complain of being hypersomnolent by day and unable to sleep at night. Hypnotics with a short duration of action should be taken in the evening to re-establish a normal rhythm. Suitable examples include zolpidem and temazepam.

Restless legs

Between 20% and 40% of patients at stage 5 CKD suffer from uraemia-associated restless legs syndrome. It can be distressing and debilitating for some patients. Restless legs syndrome is associated with anaemia and low ferritin levels which should therefore be corrected where this is feasible (IV iron and erythropoietin; see Chapter 11).

Medications such as clonazepam or temazepam are often effective. If not, pramipexole or ropinirole is the next step, titrating the dose upwards until relief is obtained. Some patients report relief from the use of gabapentin.

Muscle cramps

These are common in patients with stage 5 CKD. Quinine sulphate taken regularly may improve symptoms in some patients. For acute spasms, benzodiazepines such as diazepam and oxazepam may be effective, albeit with a risk of sedation. Methocarbamol may be used, but its efficacy is not well established.

The terminal phase

Agitation in the terminal phase can be managed with medazolam 2.5mg s/c as required, changing to a syringe driver if necessary. Glycopyrronium 0.2mg s/c as required is used to reduce respiratory tract secretions. For nausea, haloperidol is used initially s/c, changing to a syringe driver if necessary.

A patient with deteriorating kidney function who chooses not to have dialysis has an average survival time of 6.3 months. In those who withdraw from dialysis, the average time to death is eight days. From the results of various surveys, patients with renal disease and their families believe a 'good death' will be free from pain, peaceful and brief, with loved ones present and in a place of their choosing. To achieve this end, detailed and skilled palliative care planning in the terminal phase of CKD is paramount. If well-managed, uraemia is one of the least distressing ways to die.

Key points

- Implicit in a decision to opt for conservative management is the need to ask questions about an end-of-life plan.
- A well planned death from uraemia can be a positive experience for patient, family and carers.
- Communication is the key. Families must be kept informed of care plans and be involved in guiding management.
- The Liverpool Care Pathway provides specific advice relevant to managing patients dying from kidney failure (see reference below).

References and further reading

Chambers, E.J., Germain, M., & Brown, E. (eds) (2004). *Supportive Care for the Renal Patient.* Oxford: Oxford University Press.

Department of Health. (2005). National Service Framework for Renal Services - Part Two: Chronic Kidney Disease, Acute Renal Failure and End of Life Care. www.dh.gov.uk

Department of Health. (2008). Guidelines for Liverpool Care Pathway (LCP) drug prescribing in advanced chronic kidney disease. www.dh.gov.uk

Murtagh, F., Addington-Hall, J., & Higginson, I. (2007). The prevalence of symptoms in end-stage renal disease: a systematic review. *Advances in Chronic Kidney Disease* **14** (1), 82–99

19

Management and referral: A quick reference summary

This chapter draws together the information contained in the preceding chapters into a management plan that is applicable to patients. This is not condensed into a single algorithm containing all the management pathways for CKD, as doing this would oversimplify the issues discussed earlier. It would also be contrary to the stated purpose of this book, which is to offer an understanding of the various management options so that the non-specialist can make an informed decision on the best course of action for an individual patient.

Table 19.1 *Indications for renal ultrasound.*
(Adapted from NICE 2008)

Offer a renal ultrasound to all people with CKD who:

- Have progressive CKD (see definition in Chapter 10)

- Have pain that might be renal in origin

- Have visible or persistent invisible haematuria

- Have symptoms of urinary tract obstruction

- Have a family history of polycystic kidney disease and are aged over 20

- Have stage 4 or 5 CKD

Advise people with a family history of inherited kidney disease about the implications of an abnormal result before a renal ultrasound scan is arranged for them.

Table 19.2 *Criteria for referral of patients with CKD for a specialist opinion. (Adapted from NICE 2008)*

> **People with CKD in the following groups should normally be referred for specialist assessment:**
> - Stage 4 and 5 CKD (with or without diabetes)
> - Heavy proteinuria (ACR>70mg/mmol or PCR>100mg/mmol) unless known to be due to diabetes and already appropriately treated
> - Proteinuria (ACR>30mg/mmol or PCR>50 mg/mmol) together with haematuria
> - Rapidly declining eGFR (more than 5ml/min/1.73m^2 in one year, or more than 10ml/min/1.73m^2 within five years)
> - Hypertension that remains poorly controlled despite the use of at least four antihypertensive drugs at therapeutic doses
> - People with, or suspected of having, rare or genetic causes of CKD
> - Suspected renal artery stenosis (e.g. decline in eGFR after treatment with angiotensin converting enzyme inhibitors)

Table 19.3 *How levels of proteinuria measured by ACR and PCR (see Chapter 5) affect management in non-diabetic patients with eGFR<60ml/min. (Adapted from NICE 2008)*

Level of proteinuria	Action to be taken	Target BP
ACR<30mg/mmol PCR<50mg/mmol	Control BP according to NICE guidelines for managing hypertension (2011)	120–140/90
ACR 30–70mg/mmol PCR 50–100mg/mmol	Control BP using ACE-Is and ARBs first line, even in patients over 55 years of age	120–140/90
ACR>70mg/mmol PCR>100mg/mmol	Refer (non-urgent) for specialist advice	120–130/80

Table 19.4 *The normal schedule for monitoring patients at risk of CKD or on the CKD register (adapted from NICE 2008). Note that renal function should also be measured during intercurrent illness, particularly where this may lead to dehydration. Frequency of monitoring may need to be increased if results show more rapid deterioration than previously (see Chapter 10).*

Stage of CKD	eGFR range (ml/min)	Frequency of testing
No CKD, but at risk	>60	Annually
1 and 2	>60	Annually
3a, 3b	30–59	6-monthly
4	15–29	3-monthly
5	<15	Specialist advice

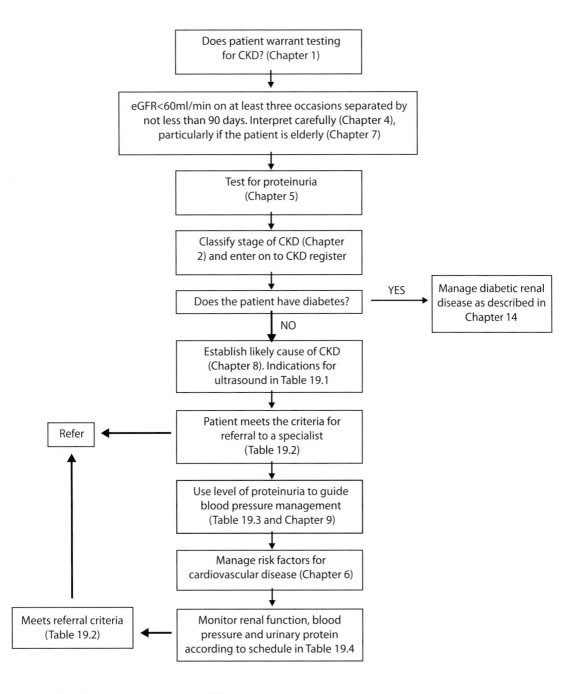

Figure 19.1 *Management algorithm for CKD.*

Index